Second Edition
Revised and Enlarged

MUCC
Published by
Michigan United Conservation Clubs
Box 30235, Lansing, Mich. 48909

Cover photo by Ben Graham

TABLE OF CONTENTS

BIG GAME

SMALL GAME

FISH

GAME BIRDS

TURTLES, FROGS AND CRAWDADS

SAUCES and STUFFINGS

MICHIGAN PLANTS

BREADS and DESSERTS

CAMP COOKING

INTRODUCTION

To the hunter and fisherman, there is nothing to compare with the joys of the chase. The sight of a loon on a lonely lake, the sound of a ruffed grouse drumming on a morning in May, the scent of the forest floor in autumn—these are the things that matter. Without them, the chase would be no more exciting than a trip to the supermarket. With them, the chase becomes a mystic and memorable excursion, even when the pursuer returns with empty creel or weightless bag.

But sometimes the creel may be heavy and the bag may bulge with the harvest of forest and field and lake and stream. On those fond occasions, the entire family comes to enjoy the chase through the bounty provided by the hunter or fisherman.

For even in this day of scientifically produced victuals there is no fare to match the savory store from nature's pantry.

Fish and game, properly cared for and properly prepared, provide us with a variety of exciting dishes, many of which are described in this unusual recipe book compiled by the staff of the Michigan United Conservation Clubs.

We know you will find this to be an invaluable reference that will enhance your enjoyment of the out-of-doors. Between these covers are literally hundreds of recipes for preparing game and fish. In this, the second edition of the book, we have expanded the number of recipes, inserted more comprehensive information on the care and preservation of fish and game, and included new sections on Michigan plants, breads and desserts which feature Michigan fruits, and campsite cooking. We would like to thank all the people from throughout the country for taking the time to write and send us their favorite recipes. We invite readers to submit recipes that might be missing from the book. Those received will be published in future editions of **The Wildlife Chef.** Send your recipes to: The Wildlife Chef, c/o Michigan United Conservation Clubs, P.O. Box 30235, Lansing, Mich. 48909.

ANTELOPE
BEAR
DEER
ELK
MOOSE

**BIG
GAME**

VENISON IS MORE THAN DEER MEAT

When a Michigan hunter thinks of "big game," he or she usually thinks of the deer he or she bagged last fall—or the one that got away. Accordingly, the focus is on recipes for deer in this section, but we also include plenty of ways to fix elk, moose, reindeer, antelope, and bear. Although the term "venison" is commonly used only in reference to deer meat, it also refers to the meat of elk, reindeer, antelope, moose, or any large, antlered animal. So, feel free to substitute these meats for each other in any recipe. You can also substitute any venison cuts for the equivalent cut of beef in any of your favorite recipes. Deer meat is much like beef, except the lean part is sweeter and the fat has a stronger taste.

AFTER THE KILL

Venison is excellent meat and should be treated with care and respect. The hunter's pride in bagging his deer should not stop after the kill, but continue through to the excellent chops and roasts he or she can serve to guests as they listen spellbound to the tale of the hunt.

EQUIPMENT. Some basic tools are essential for every hunter. A butcher's skinning knife can be used in dressing the animal and is most efficient in the skinning process. Bring along a whetstone to keep the knife sharp. A hand ax or folding saw is essential for splitting elk or moose carcasses and quartering any big game. You will also need 20 or more feet of rope to tie up the carcass, and several lengths of cheesecloth to wrap the meat and clean out the abdominal cavity.

BLEEDING. A quick, clean kill will prevent the animal's blood and adrenalin from rushing into its muscles as it bounds away wounded. After your animal is down, approach it carefully from the rear. Make sure it's dead before you get close so you don't get kicked with its sharp hooves. Bleed the carcass **immediately**; by keeping the blood from getting into the meat and tainting it, you can prevent any "gamey" taste often associated with venison.

Place the animal on a slant with its head on the ground and its hind legs high. Insert your knife at the top of the breastbone with point aimed at the backbone. Pull out the knife with a slight cutting motion. This will sever some major arteries and will drain much of the animal's blood.

While you wait for the blood to drain, cut off the musk glands on the inside and outside of each leg. A heavy patch of upraised hair growing over the glands makes them easy to find. Wash your hands and knife well to prevent the meat from smelling musky.

DRESSING. When most of the blood has drained, prop the animal on its back, using stones to keep it from rolling over. Spread the hind legs as far apart as possible. If you're alone, tie one leg to a tree to give yourself a free hand.

Take care when opening the body cavity that you don't rupture the stomach or intestines. Slit through the skin from the upper abdomen just in back of the breastbone to down and around the anus. Draw the anus into the body cavity so it will come out with the intestines. Be careful not to puncture the bladder. Roll the skin back from each side of the cut to keep hair out of the meat. Cut along the same line as before, this time through the muscles. Keep the cutting edge of the knife up and between the fingers, and follow it carefully with your other hand underneath, pushing down the entrails so they don't get cut.

When the abdominal cavity is open, roll the entrails out. Cut the membrane from the rib cage and split the breastbone partway to the neck. Reach in through the chest cavity to cut out the trachea and esophagus, after removing the lungs and heart.

Save the heart, liver and kidneys for later use. Wipe the inside of the body with a clean, dry cloth or dried grass to get rid of excess blood and loose tissue.

With all the insides out, the animal should be hung from a tree to allow it to drain completely. To hang the carcass, cut a gambrel (a short, stout pole), and slide it through the hamstrings. Tie a rope to the gambrel and hoist the animal into a tree. Prop the body cavity open with short poles to help it cool. First cut the hide around the animal's neck. Then cut along the inside of each leg from the cavity opening to the first joint. Cut the shanks 1-½'' below the hook.

Grab the pelt with one hand pulling outwards and the other forcing the pelt away from the carcass. If you plan to use the hide, salt the flesh side and roll it up for a couple days to loosen the hair. Tack it up on a wall or other flat surface, taking care not to overstretch it. Remove all flesh and tallow still on the hide. Don't fold the hide because the folds will always be visible.

COOLING. Rapid cooling is very important to insure fresh, prime meat. Taking the entrails out, wiping clean the chest and abdominal cavity, and skinning the carcass all hasten the cooling process and at the same time, make the meat easier to carry. The meat should be wrapped or peppered liberally to protect it from insects.

TRANSPORTING. When transporting your future feast back home, strap the carcass on the roof or the trunk of the car if it is cool and cloudy. It could be put inside the trunk if the lid is propped open to allow air to circulate. It's a bad idea to carry the carcass on the hood of a car because the engine heat will spoil the meat.

AGING. The meat should hang at least 24 hours before being used. It is generally agreed that venison will reach its finest flavor when hung for 10 to 14 days at a temperature between 34° and 40°F. This gives natural enzymes a chance to tenderize the meat. Aged meat is a dark red color; this color does **not** necessarily signify spoiled meat, like most people believe. Pounding meat with a heavy mallet also works to tenderize it. Try pounding flour into the meat, or mix a tablespoon of fresh ground coffee with some flour and then pound the mixture into meat for a new flavor.

BUTCHERING, FREEZING, COOKING

BUTCHERING. Cutting the carcass into pieces for cooking or preserving isn't difficult if you have the proper equipment, a place to work, and some knowledge of how to proceed. If you lack any one of these, it will probably be much easier and much more

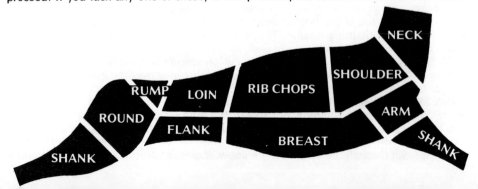

satisfactory to have a professional butcher do the job. This will certainly be the case if you have your deer frozen, and refrigerator storage is about the best way to preserve venison.

If you decide to cut up the carcass yourself, the first step is to remove the hide. Then hang the carcass by the hocks with a spreader and saw it in half down the backbone with a common handsaw. Take half of the carcass at a time, and cut it using a sharp knife, saw, or cleaver. Cut all discolored, bloodshot parts off the pieces, soak them in salt water overnight, and use them immediately.

CUTS OF VENISON

Hind and fore shanks are good for soups, stews and ground for meat loaf and deerburgers.

Cut the round in slices 2 inches thick; it is usually tender and makes delicious steaks. If it happens to be tough, it may be used for Swiss steak. When the leg is small it may be roasted all in one piece in an uncovered pan. Round may also be ground and used like ground beef.

Loin is where you get sirloin, porterhouse steaks, or choice roasts. Cut rib steaks at least 1-½ inches thick.

The shoulder, or chuck, makes good pot roast or ground meat. It may also be corned or canned. Be sure to follow canning directions exactly to prevent food poisoning.

Rump makes a good pot roast. If it's from a tender young buck, it is delicious baked uncovered in the oven. It can also be corned or canned. Each rump roast will usually produce two roasts large enough to feed a family of four.

The neck is tender after the tendons are removed. It may be used in a stew or as ground meat, and even makes good roasts.

The flank and breast contain considerable meat. It may be ground or used for soup or stew.

FREEZER TIPS

There are several ways to make your freezer more efficient, which saves money and energy at the same time.

1. Check the location of the freezer. Every type of refrigerator or freezer has a warm air outlet which must be kept clear. If the freezer is too close to a wall, for example, the warm air outlet may be blocked. This will cause overheating and long, laborious operation of the cooling unit, giving you an unnecessarily high electricity bill.

2. Make sure the freezer is out of the direct path of any heat source, such as a warm air register or sunlight.

3. Be sure the door of the unit is airtight. A good test is to close it on a piece of paper. If the paper comes out easily, cold air is leaking out, and the door gasket should be replaced or the door latch readjusted.

4. Open the door as little as possible. Know what you want and where it's located before you open the door.

5. If you have a manual defrost freezer make sure that ice never builds up to more than ¼ inch inside. Frost and ice cut cooling power.

6. Keep lint and dust off the condensor coil, which is usually located in back of the base plate or in the rear of the unit.

7. The unit must be level to operate quietly.

8. When you put large amounts of unfrozen food into the freezer, turn the control to a colder setting for fast freezing. When the new food is frozen, turn the temperature control back to its normal setting.

9. Do not put uncovered liquids in a frost-free refrigerator.

10. When the refrigerator will remain closed for a long period of time, for example during a vacation, turn the temperature control one or two points warmer. Many of the

newer model refrigerators have a "Vacation Setting" which essentially does the same thing.

11. A well-packed freezer, used to at least four-fifths capacity, operates most efficiently.

FREEZER STORAGE

To wrap meat, fish, or game birds, use only moisture and vapor-proof materials, such as aluminum foil, polyethylene bags, freezer film wraps, plastic and metal containers. Divide meat into individual servings. Separate the servings with two layers of wax paper, and in each package put enough servings for a meal for your family. Wrap the package tightly, pressing the paper or foil into hollows to push out all the air possible, and fasten it with freezer tape.

Be sure to label your packages as to the type of meat, the cut, the number of servings, the weight, and the date. Freeze no more than three pounds per cubic foot of freezer space within 24 hours. Venison and game birds can be kept 8 to 12 months frozen solidly. Duck and turkey will keep 6 months, as will fresh-frozen lean fish. Fatter fish, like salmon, should be eaten within 2 to 3 months.

Meat frozen at 0°F or below will retain the freshness and quality it had before freezing. Freezing does not improve the flavor but merely slows down the degenerative process. The lower the temperature, the slower the loss of quality. Five degrees F should be the maximum freezer temperature.

When you are ready to cook your catch, take it out of the freezer the night before and thaw it in the refrigerator. This prevents moisture loss and allows the center of the meat to thaw without allowing the outside to reach dangerously high bacteria levels. Meat, fish and poultry can be cooked without thawing if you allow ⅓ to ½ more cooking time.

Plain meat, fish and poultry may be refrozen if it has been partially thawed, but it must still contain ice crystals and still be firm in the center. If the meat has thawed completely or warmed to room temperature, it should be cooked immediately or discarded.

COOKING TIPS

Venison's natural flavor is sweeter than other meat, so reduce the sugar in sauce recipes by about one-fourth.

Acids can be used to tenderize the meat. Vinegar, tomato sauce and French dressing sauces complement the flavor of venison. Cover the meat and let it stand in the marinating sauce for at least 24 hours, then broil.

Take care not to overcook venison. It has short fibers that toughen quickly if it's overcooked at too high a temperature. Venison is best when it's medium to well-done; never serve it rare or overdone.

Venison should be served hot because deer fat tends to congeal while it is still warm.

Use left-overs in hash, stew, or soup.

JERKY

Jerky is dried meat, cut in strips an inch thick and sun dried. It is easy to carry and lasts a long time without refrigeration.

Half-frozen meat is easier to slice for jerky. For crunchy jerky, cut with the grain and in fairly thin strips; for chewier jerky, cut thicker strips against the grain. Trim off all fat as it creates a rancid taste.

Here are several methods to make jerky.

First, for sun-dried jerky, cut fresh meat into long thin strips an inch wide and an inch thick. After rubbing the meat with salt, hang it on racks in the sun to dry. Store the jerky in sacks hung in a dry place.

A second method uses a brine solution and a smokehouse. Cut lean strips of venison into pieces 1 to 1½ inches thick and 6 inches long. Any cut of meat can be used, but tender meat produces a better product. Make a brine of half a pound of salt to each gallon of water, storing it in a granite container, stone crock, or plastic bucket. Put in the meat, and weight it so the liquid covers the surface. Let it stand at least twelve hours.

Drain well and place on trays from a smokehouse. (See the "How to Smoke Fish" section in the chapter on Fish for instructions on how to build a smokehouse.) Dry out the meat in the smokehouse, and flavor it with warm, not hot, smoke for 5 to 15 days, depending on the size of the pieces. Use any non-resinous wood, like maple, oak, ash, or apple. Store the jerky in airtight containers. It will keep indefinitely if all the fat has been removed before brining.

Jerky can also be made in the oven. Slice the meat half an inch thick and remove all fat. Lay the meat out in a single layer on a counter surface. Make a solution of ½ teaspoon liquid smoke to 2 tablespoons water, and dab this on each piece with a brush. Salt generously and pepper if you like. Place the strips layer on layer in a large bowl or crock. Put a plate on top of the meat. Let it stand at least six hours.

Remove the meat strips from the bowl and dry them. Remove the racks from your oven, and stretch meat strips across the racks, allowing edges to touch but not overlap. There must be room for air circulation in the oven, so don't cover the whole rack. Arrange the racks so the top rack is no closer than four inches from the top source of heat, and the bottom rack is no closer than four inches from the bottom of the oven. Keep the meat in the oven for 11 hours at 150 degrees. Early in the drying, check the meat. If there is an excessive drip, catch it on aluminum foil on a rack near the bottom of the oven. After the meat is dry, cool it and store it in an airtight container.

BEAR

Bear should be killed in the early fall for best eating. It should be skinned and cleaned out immediately or else the hide and entrails will give the meat a strong flavor. Soak the meat for at least ten hours in cold water to remove any strong taste and to clean up the meat. After it has been soaked, the preparation will be the same as for pork in either roasting or frying. It is a carrier of trichinosis, like pork, so it should be cooked to a well-done state.

 VENISON

Camp Cooked Chops

center cut chops cut thick
salt
pepper
½ cup chopped onions
1-2 cans of beer
freshly gathered sweet fern (This is not a real fern, but a short twiggy plant with fragrant, finely cut leaves, Myrica asplenifolia, to be exact. It is found near almost all north Michigan fishing areas.)

Place the chops in a pan wide enough to accommodate all chops and leave room for turning. Season both sides with salt and pepper, onions and the fern. Pour over the chops one can of beer. The liquid should nearly cover the chops; water may be added unless you can spare another can of beer. Allow chops to marinate, turning occasionally for several hours or all day if the camp pets don't get into the chops. Cook on grill over steady heat about 15 minutes per side, or until appropriately charred.

Serve with your favorite salad, hard rolls and perhaps camp fried potatoes. Also beer.

Braised Antelope Chops

Dredge antelope chops in seasoned flour, brown in hot fat. Pour over them 1 can of beef broth and one small package dried onion soup mix. Simmer until almost dry. Remove meat, and make gravy from the drippings.

Japanese Ribs

4 pounds venison ribs
½ cup soy sauce, Japanese style
½ cup cooking sherry (may omit)
½ cup water
4 tablespoons brown sugar
2 cloves garlic, crushed

Preheat oven to 350 degrees. Arrange racks of ribs in a large roasting pan. Combine all ingredients. Stir well and pour over ribs. Cover pan. Bake 45 minutes, turning ribs once or twice. Remove cover and continue cooking until golden brown and well done. Baste with sauce or turn ribs occasionally. For crispy brown ribs, try to arrange in roaster in single layer.

Charcoal-broiled Chops or Steaks

Brush meat well with cooking oil. Sprinkle with garlic salt and put on a rack in the broiler or on the outdoor grill. Cook a short time on each side. Do not let the meat dry out. Spread hot steaks with ½ cup lemon butter with 1 tablespoon parsley flakes added.

Fresh Steak

Fresh steak can be good if properly prepared.

Cut steaks 1 inch thick. Put between waxed paper and flatten with a mallet or side of a cleaver until ¼ inch thick. Have frying pan hot. Put in 1 tablespoon of butter. Drop in the steaks, but keep shaking the pan so steak does not stick. Salt and pepper lightly, while cooking. Turn just once, all the time shaking the pan. Serve hot with butter on top. The entire process takes about 3 minutes.

Steaks will be rare, but tender and delicious.

Pan-Fried Venison Steaks

Serves 4
1 pound "ham" steaks, ½" thick
¼ cup thick cream or evaporated milk
¼ cup flour
3 teaspoons butter
salt and pepper to taste

Pound steaks thoroughly with sharp-edged meat pounder. Cut into serving pieces. Dip steaks into cream and dredge in flour. Brown one side in hot butter.

Turn, salt and pepper to taste. Continue browning until second side is well-browned.

Burgundy Venison Steak Tips

Serves 6-8
2 lbs. venison steak, cut in small cubes
3 tablespoons oil
2 tablespoons dry onion soup mix (more if you want)
3 beef bouillon cubes
2 cups water
1 cup burgundy wine
1 cup fresh mushrooms or 4 oz. canned

Brown meat in hot oil. Add remaining ingredients and simmer for about 1 hour. Add mushrooms the last 5 minutes. Serve over fluffy rice.

Catawba County Wildlife Club • Joan Wilfong

Venison Stroganoff

Serves 6-8
Cut 2 pounds of round steak into small cubes. Roll in flour, salt and pepper and brown in hot butter. Add ½ cup water and ½ cup vinegar and simmer until tender. Add water as necessary to keep from burning. When tender, pour off excess liquid. Add:
1 cup sour cream
1 bay leaf
pepper to taste
1 small can mushroom pieces
4 tablespoons butter
2 teaspoons celery salt
2 tablespoons Worcestershire sauce

Cover, simmer until everything is heated through. Don't boil. Serve over brown rice or noodles.

Japanese Venison

Serves 4
Cut venison steaks into very thin strips. Slice 3 large onions into ¼ inch slices. Make about ¼ pound of meat strips for each person. This recipe is for four persons.

Make sauce by mixing:
1 cup soy sauce
2 pieces crushed garlic
¼ teaspoon Accent

Cook meat and onion over charcoal until done—only a minute or so.

Cook onions with the meat.

Serve each person a dish with some sauce, and let them dip their cooked meat strips and onions, piping hot, into the sauce for eating.

Teriyaki Steak

2 pounds venison steak, cut thin
1 can beef consomme (undiluted)
⅓ cup soy sauce
1 teaspoon savor salt
2 tablespoons lemon juice
2 tablespoons brown sugar
¼ cup chopped green onions (including tops)
1 clove garlic

Cut the steak diagonally, across the grain. Mix the other ingredients to form a marinating sauce. Pour the sauce over the meat strips and refrigerate overnight. Drain and broil 4″ from heat until tender. Do not overcook.

Venison Sauerbraten

Serves 4-6
2 pounds venison chuck, round or rump roast
1 cup vinegar
6 peppercorns
5 whole bay leaves
water to cover
3 tablespoons fat
6 carrots
6 onions
1 cup sliced celery
1 tablespoon sugar
10 gingersnaps, crushed

Trim all visible fat from venison. Place in glass dish with cover. Add peppercorns, cloves and bay leaves to vinegar and pour over meat. Add enough water to cover meat. Cover dish and refrigerate for at least 5 days.

Remove meat from marinade. Reserve the liquid for gravy. Heat fat in heavy frying pan. Brown meat on both sides, add vegetables and 2 cups marinade. Simmer until meat and vegetables are tender, approximately 1½ hours. Remove meat and vegetables from pan. Add sugar and gingersnaps to remaining liquid to make gravy.

Venison Pasties

Serves 4
Works well with beef, too:
Pastry for 9″, 2 crust pie
¾ pound venison round, cut into small cubes
2 potatoes, diced
2 carrots, thinly sliced
3 tablespoons minced onions
1 teaspoon salt
¼ teaspoon pepper
¼-½ teaspoon dried thyme
2 tablespoons chopped fresh parsley
4 teaspoons water

Roll out half of pie dough and place in a 9″ pie plate. Mix venison and remaining ingredients. Place half of mixture on pie dough in pie plate. Fold dough over filling to make half-moon shape that fills half of the pie plate. Seal and crimp edges. Do not slit dough. You will have 2 half-pies or pasties. Bake at 375 degrees for 1 hour and 10 minutes. Pierce crust and vegetables with a sharp fork to be sure vegetables are tender.

Venison Swiss Steak

2½ pounds venison
½ teaspoon salt
½ cup flour
dash of pepper
2 tablespoons butter or margarine
½ cup green pepper, chopped
½ cup chopped onions
1½ cup water
1 small can tomato paste
1 tablespoon bead molasses

Trim all fat from venison. Roll meat in salt, pepper and flour. Brown meat in margarine in frying pan. Add water, tomato paste, bead molasses, green peppers and onions. Bring to a simmer, stirring frequently. Lower temperature and let simmer for about 2 hours, stirring occasionally. Serve piping hot with boiled parsley potatoes.

Stuffed Moose Steak

1 boned moose steak
flour, seasoned with salt & pepper
3 cups croutons
¾ cup onion, chopped
¾ cup celery, chopped
½ cup butter
½ teaspoon paprika
1 green pepper, sliced
sliced bacon

Dredge steak in flour, salt and pepper and pound well on both sides. Mix rest of ingredients, except bacon, to make a stuffing and place on the steak. Roll up and tie. Set rolled steak in roasting pan. Place slices of bacon over steaks.

Roast in 325 degrees F oven until tender.

Cornish Elk Pasties

Serves 5
Crust for 5 pasties:
3 cups flour
1 teaspoon salt
1 cup lard
1 cup cold water

Sift flour and salt twice. Cut in lard until pieces are size of small peas. Add water a little at a time. Toss until mixture holds together, handling as little as possible. Cut into 5 portions. Roll out each portion on floured board the size of a 9-inch pie tin.

Filling:
Rutabaga, grated
Potatoes, cubed
flank steak (elk), cubed
fresh pork, cubed
salt and pepper
suet, finely chopped
onion, minced
potatoes, diced

For 1 pasty:
Grate 2 tablespoons of rutabaga on dough. Add ¾ cup of cubed potatoes (½'' x 1/8''). Add 3 oz. of flank steak and 1 oz. of fresh pork which have been cut into cubes ½'' square. Add salt and pepper to taste. Sprinkle 1 teaspoon finely chopped suet over meat. Add 1 tablespoon minced onion. Add 2 tablespoons diced potatoes. Fold crust over and crinkle edge to seal. Cut slit in top of each pastry to allow steam to escape. Bake at 400 degrees F 1 hour.

Antelope Barbecue

Sear 3 pounds of antelope steaks in frying pan with slices of salt pork or other fat. Mix the following ingredients in saucepan:
1 cup catsup
1 tablespoon salt
3 slices lemon
1 onion sliced thin
⅓ cup beef steak sauce
2 tablespoons tarragon vinegar
1 tablespoon chili powder (or hot sauce)

Bring mixture to a boil—stir to avoid burning. Cover venison with the sauce and roast in moderate oven (350 degrees F). Cook 1½ hours turning occasionally.

Harter's Venison Roast

Make liquid of half vinegar and half water, (total 1 quart). Add 1 tablespoon salt, 8 bay leaves, and 8 whole cloves. Let roast stand in this 24 hours. Stab meat with a pick to help liquid penetrate. Remove all fat. Rinse and dry—firm up in the refrigerator. Salt and pepper. Cut suet from beef and bacon strips 3'' long and ¼'' wide. Stick pointed knife into meat—push forward on blade, making an opening on back of it. Push suet and bacon as far down as you can. Do this every square inch of the roast. Now, completely cover top of roast with bacon and suet. Place in roasting pan with ¼'' water in the bottom.

Bake at 325 degrees until tender. It takes at least 25 minutes per pound. Keep water level to ¼'' and baste frequently. May roast vegetables with it.

Roast Whole Leg of Venison

Rub well with salt and pepper. Lard with strips of salt pork. Surround with carrots, potatoes and onions. Roast uncovered at 300 degrees for about 20 minutes per pound. Baste frequently with dry or cooking sherry.

Tom Washington

Roast Venison with Golden Gravy

4-5 pounds venison shoulder roast, or other roast portion from a deer
2 cans Campbells Golden Mushroom soup
Small potatoes and carrots
1 package Liptons onion soup
Worchestershire sauce
Seasonings to taste, (Lawreys salt, onion, and/or garlic salts, black pepper)

Clean all fat and membrane from meat, then soak meat in cold water several hours.

Wipe meat dry, then rub liberally with the Worchestershire sauce and season with the seasonings. Allow to marinate several hours at room temperature. This roast can be cooked in a large electric fry pan, or in the oven, at 350 degrees. Brown meat well on all sides, in a mixture of cooking oil and oleo, then remove meat, and drain fry pan of excess grease. Cover the bottom of fry pan with one inch of hot water, and simmer the "goodies" from bottom of pan.

Blend in the Campbells Golden Mushroom and Liptons onion soups, and simmer to a smooth consistency. (Make sure you use the Golden Mushroom soup, not Cream of Mushroom, so you obtain the unique gravy flavor).

Place meat into the pan, and set temperature at 350 degrees. While meat has started cooking peel potatoes and carrots, and arrange around meat. Spoon the gravy mixture over everything, cover and cook two to three hours. Baste about every half hour, and thin gravy with water, if it should start sticking to bottom of pan.

When ready to serve, remove meat and vegetables to platters, and thicken gravy with flour and water mixture, to desired consistency. Serve bubbling hot at the table, so your hungry guests can spoon liberal amounts over their meat. Served with a tossed salad, this makes one of the most delicious wild game meals you could enjoy eating.

This recipe can be used to prepare almost any wild game, including rabbit, pheasant, partridge, squirrel and duck, following the same general directions.

Sauerbraten

Serves 8
  Mix:
2 cups vinegar
2 cups red wine
4 cups water
2 large onions, sliced
3 tablespoons salt
1 sliced lemon
10 whole cloves
5 bay leaves
5 whole peppercorns
1 tablespoon parsley, chopped
1 teaspoon allspice

Place 5 pound rump roast in large bowl, add mixture and let the meat stand 36 hours, turning occasionally. Remove meat and brown it in hot fat. Add 1 cup of seasoning mixture, cover tightly and cook slowly until tender. Add a little water if necessary.

Barbecued Venison Ham

Rub ham or leg of deer, elk, etc. with lots of salt, pepper and onion salt. This can be done while the meat is frozen and allowed to sit with the salt until it thaws.

Bake for an hour in a medium oven and then put in an enclosed outdoor grill at 200 degrees. Add green hickory wood to the charcoal in the grill. Turn occasionally and baste with barbecue sauce until done (about 3 hours).

Barbecued Venison #1

1 (28 oz.) bottle prepared barbecue sauce
1 cup catsup
2 tablespoons pickle relish
1 cup beef broth or pan juice from venison roast
1 small onion, chopped
2 stalks celery, chopped
2 pounds cooked rump roast, of venison

Mix all ingredients except venison in large saucepan. Cook over low heat for about 30 minutes or until sauce is thick. Slice rump roast into the bubbling sauce and simmer until meat is just heated through. Makes 5 servings of 2 hearty sandwiches per person.

Barbecued Venison #2

2 onions, chopped
6 tablespoons salad oil
2 tablespoons sugar
2 teaspoons dry mustard
2 teaspoons paprika
1 cup water
½ cup vinegar
2 tablespoons Worcestershire sauce
2 drops tobasco sauce, optional
slice, cooked venison

Brown onions in salad oil. Add remaining ingredients except venison. Arrange meat in casserole. Pour sauce over meat. Bake at 375 degrees F for 20 minutes, or until sauce thickens.

Elk Burgundy

6-7 pound leg of elk (remove bone if using the shank)
2 cups burgundy
1 cup beef bouillon
1 medium onion, sliced
1 clove garlic, crushed
1 bay leaf
1 teaspoon salt
6 slices bacon
3 juniper berries (optional)

Combine all ingredients except meats. Simmer on the stove for 15 minutes until flavor is blended. Let marinade cool. Set meat in ceramic bowl and cover with marinade. Marinate for 24 hours, turning occasionally, in the refrigerator.

Take meat out and pat dry. Roll and tie. Place bacon strips across roast. Bake uncovered at 450 degrees for 10 minutes. Reduce heat to 325 degrees F and roast 15-18 minutes per pound. Baste meat with strained marinade. Make gravy from the drippings, using more marinade for the liquid.

Rolled Antelope Roast

Serves 1-6

4 pounds of antelope (use rump cut or top of round, rolled and tied)

salt & pepper

Try to use at least a four pound roast since venison shrinks during cooking. Place meat in conventional roasting pan but do not cover or add water. Bacon strips may be toothpicked onto the roast for basting juices, or you may use liquid shortening to baste. Roast in low oven, 300 degrees F. (Low temperature retards shrinkage). Frequently baste with bacon fat or liquid shortening.

Allow 32-35 minutes cooking time for each pound of roast.

Antelope & Wine

5 pound roast

1 cup dry red wine

1 cup melted butter

4 tablespoons rosemary

Baste the roast with melted butter. Set in an open roaster and sprinkle rosemary all over the roast. Add the red wine. Roast at 350 degrees. Add water when the wine begins to turn dark brown. Baste frequently. Cook until meat is brown and tender, about 30 minutes to the pound.

Venison On the Table

1 large lemon

2 sprigs parsley

2 carrots

2 tablespoons vinegar

2 tablespoons Angostura bitters

1 cup flat beer

2 teaspoons coarse ground pepper

1 teaspoon salt

2 tablespoons salad oil

Slice the lemon, then grate the carrot. Put these and remaining ingredients in a deep, flat bottomed dish (not plastic). Place venison or other meat in the marinade so it is completely covered. The marinade should be enough for a four pound venison roast. Stir occasionally and turn several times during this marinating period—24 to 48 hours. When the meat is through marinating, place the roast in a preheated 350° oven for three hours. Salt the meat well when you begin the roasting, then baste it every 30 minutes with the marinade. The bitters take the place of spices and the beer helps to assure a tender and non-gamey taste.

Margaret L. Baldini • Grants Pass, Oregon

Barbecued Deerburgers

Serves 8-10

For strong, gamey meat:

3 tablespoons fat or drippings

2 pounds ground venison

1 cup onion, chopped

1 cup celery, finely diced

½ large green pepper, chopped fine

1 clove garlic, minced

½ cup chili sauce

½ cup ketchup

2 tablespoons chopped parsley

1¾ cup water

2 teaspoons salt

¼ teaspoon pepper

2 tablespoons Worcestershire sauce

¼ cup vinegar

1 tablespoon brown sugar

2 teaspoons dry mustard

1 teaspoon paprika

2 teaspoons chili powder

Preheat fry pan. Add fat and melt. When hot, add meat, onions and celery. Brown, stirring frequently. Spoon off excess fat. Combine remaining ingredients, except parsley. Mix well and pour over meat. Cover fry pan and simmer 30 minutes, stirring occasionally. Add parsley, serve between hot buns or over mashed potatoes, rice or noodles.

Deerburger Skillet Meal

1 tablespoon butter

½ pound ground venison

½ medium onion, chopped

½ green pepper, chopped

1 cup tomatoes, canned

½ tablespoon Worcestershire sauce

½ teaspoon salt

1/16 teaspoon pepper

¾ cup water

3 ounces noodles

Melt butter in fry pan. Add ground venison. Stir to brown the meat. Add chopped onion and green pepper and continue cooking until onion is light brown. Add all ingredients except noodles. Stir and heat to boiling. Spread uncooked noodles over the top. Cover tightly. Simmer for 15 minutes or until noodles are tender and have absorbed most of the liquid.

Meat Balls

2 pounds ground venison
2 teaspoons salt
¼ teaspoon pepper
1 onion chopped fine
1 cup celery, chopped
2 tablespoons shortening
½ cup green pepper, chopped
4 eggs, slightly beaten
1 cup cracker crumbs, crushed
tomato juice or sauce

Mix ground venison, salt and pepper, onion, celery, green pepper, eggs and cracker crumbs. Shape into small balls and brown in shortening. Pour tomato sauce or tomato juice over the meat balls. Cover and allow to simmer for about 1 hour.

Venison and Rice Casserole

lard or suet
2 pounds ground venison
salt & pepper
2 cups celery, diced
2 cups onion, diced
1 green pepper, diced
1 can mushroom soup
1 can chicken and rice soup
1 cup uncooked rice

Melt lard or suet in large fry pan. Add venison, salt, pepper, celery, onion and green pepper and cook until brown. Combine remaining ingredients and pour over meat and vegetables. Simmer for 1 hour at 300 degrees F.

Venison and Corn Casserole

Serves 8
1 pound ground venison
4 celery stalks, diced
2 medium onions, chopped
1 can (10½ oz.) tomato soup
1 can (1 pound) cream-style corn
1 can (15½ oz.) kidney beans, drained
1 teaspoon garlic salt
dash pepper
1½ tablespoon Worcestershire sauce
1 teaspoon chili sauce
1 package (3¾ oz.) corn chips

Heat oven to 375 degrees F. Brown ground venison in large, heavy skillet. Add celery and onions. Cook and stir 3 minutes. Reduce heat. Stir in soup, corn, beans and seasonings. Pour into 2 quart casserole. Bake uncovered 20 minutes. Top with corn chips. Bake 10-15 minutes, or until chips are slightly toasted.

Variation: Omit corn chips. Bake 35 minutes and serve with corn bread.

Meat Loaf

1 pound ground venison neck, shank, flank, shoulder
½ pound ground pork
1 egg
½ cup dried bread crumbs
1 tablespoon chopped onion
1½ teaspoon salt
1 cup milk

Beat the egg, add milk and bread crumbs. Mix thoroughly with the meat and seasoning. Put in loaf pan.

Mix:
½ cup prepared mustard
½ cup ketchup
2 tablespoons brown sugar

Spread over top of the meat loaf. Bake in medium oven (350 degrees F) for 1 hour. Pour off excess grease if necessary.

Meat loaf may be made with all venison, but addition of pork makes a more tender loaf.

Venison Pie

Brown 1 pound ground venison and also 1 medium onion. When brown, add 1 can (1 cup) of corn, 1 cup green beans, and 1 can (1 cup) of tomato soup or preserved tomatoes without the juice. Mix together. Season.

Put in casserole and top with mashed potatoes. Grated cheese, parsley, or paprika may be used for garnish. Bake in oven at 350 degrees F for 35-40 minutes.

This may also be put in a regular pie crust. If that is done, dice potatoes and add to original mixture.

Jeannine Staneway • Lansing

Venison Chili

Brown 1 pound of ground venison and 1 large onion in oil. Depending on the fat content of venison, shortening may be added. Add 2 quarts of canned tomatoes or 2 large cans of tomatoes, 1 can kidney beans and chili powder to taste. Simmer 2 hours.

Jeannine Staneway • Lansing

Poyha

This is a meatloaf recipe handed down by the Cherokee Indians:

1 pound ground venison
1 No. 303 can whole kernel corn
1 small onion, chopped
1 teaspoon salt
2 eggs
½ cup cornmeal
½ cup water

Measure the cornmeal and place in a small bowl. Add the water and stir to mix. Allow to stand. Brown the venison in fat. When meat is thoroughly cooked add the corn and onion. Cook 10 minutes. Add the salt, egg and cornmeal. Stir well. Cook another 15 minutes, then put in a greased loaf pan and bake 30-45 minutes at 350 degrees F. Serve with cheese sauce or mushroom soup.

Deerburger Soup

Serves 8

1-2 pounds deerburger
1 cup onion, diced
1 cup raw potatoes, cubed
1 cup carrots, sliced
1 cup cabbage, shredded
¼ cup rice
beef concentrate to taste
1 small bay leaf
½ teaspoon thyme
2 teaspoons salt
1/8 teaspoon pepper
1½ quarts water
1 No. 2 can tomatoes

Brown deerburger and onion in large kettle. Add potatoes, carrots and cabbage. Bring to boil. Sprinkle rice into mixture. Add remaining ingredients, except tomatoes. Cover and simmer for 1 hour. Add tomatoes, just before serving. Skim off fat, if necessary.

Smoked Moose Sausage

1 pound of ground lean moose meat
1 teaspoon salt
⅓ pound ground pork
¼ teaspoon black pepper
¼ teaspoon ground thyme
¼ teaspoon sage
¼ teaspoon garlic salt
¼ cup water

Mix all ingredients together and stuff into casings. Sausage may be smoked for 8 hours before simmering 15-20 minutes.

Meatza Pie

1 pound ground moose meat
⅔ cup evaporated milk
½ cup fine dry bread crumbs
1 teaspoon garlic salt
⅓ cup tomato paste or catsup
1 (2 oz.) can sliced mushrooms
1 cup shredded sharp Cheddar cheese
¼ teaspoon oregano, crumbled
2 tablespoons grated Parmesan cheese

Place meat, milk, bread crumbs and garlic salt in 9-inch pie plate. Mix together with a fork. Pat this mixture evenly onto bottom and sides of pie plate, and press firmly with fingers into place. Spread tomato paste over meat mixture. Drain mushrooms and arrange over paste. Top with shredded sharp cheese and over this sprinkle oregano. Complete with 2 table-spoons or more of Parmesan cheese. Bake at 375 degrees for 25 minutes, or until meat is done to your taste and cheese lightly browned.

Mrs. Carl Sisson • Hebo, Oregon

Mulligan

Into large casserole (or Dutch oven) put:

½ onion, chopped (in bottom of pan)
¼ cup rice (raw), sprinkled through onions
2 big potatoes, sliced and put on top
1 pound ground venison, spread on top
salt and pepper
1 can (medium) pork and beans (on top of ground beef)
1 can tomato juice (large, poured over all; poke around so it soaks through to onions and rice).

Pop in oven and bake, covered, about 1-½ hours at 350°. (Can also use electric fry pan—it is faster).

Eleanor Makinster • Rainier, Oregon

Deer Vatapa

1 pound deer tenderloin, ground fine
¼ pound shredded coconut
1 bay leaf
1 green pepper, chopped fine
½ cup roasted peanuts, ground very fine
yellow cornmeal
1 tablespoon olive oil
½ pound sausage
1 small onion, chopped
1 clove garlic, mashed
7 cups water
½ teaspoon salt

Cook onion, garlic, bay leaf, green pepper, olive oil in 2 cups of water for 5 minutes. Season with salt. Add deer meat. Cover. Simmer 15 minutes. Strain broth. Set aside. Add coconut to 5 cups water and bring to boil. Simmer a few minutes. Add ground nuts and sausage. Simmer a few minutes longer. Add broth. Bring to a boil. Add deer meat. Stir in enough cornmeal to make a smooth thick mush. Cook 30 minutes. Keep stirring to prevent burning.

Tortilla Casserole

Brown together 1 pound ground venison and 1 onion. Drain excess grease and add 1 10-oz. bottle enchilada sauce. Simmer 20 minutes.

Mix together 1 large container small curd cottage cheese, 2 eggs and 1 tablespoon parsley. Shred ½ pound Monterey Jack cheese and ½ cup Cheddar cheese. Layer tostadas (these are pre-packaged and cooked like taco shells), meat mixture, cottage cheese, and Monterey Jack cheese. Keep layering as you would lasagne. Put the Cheddar cheese on top. Sprinkle crushed tortilla chips around edge of casserole. Bake at 350° until bubbly, about ½ hour.

Betty Lou Wulkan • MUCC

Venison Salami

Mix thoroughly:
5 pounds ground venison
5 rounded teaspoons Morton's "Tender Quick" salt
2½ teaspoons mustard seed
2 teaspoons pepper
2½ teaspoons garlic salt
1 teaspoon hickory smoke salt

Refrigerate mixture for three days, taking it out to remix it at least once a day. On the fourth day, shape the mixture into small loaves, about 2½ inches round or square by 6 inches long. Put on a cookie sheet and bake overnight—10 hours at 150°.

U.P. Venison Liver

Slice liver thinly. Cover with water and bring to a boil. Pour off water. Slice 1 large onion and saute in 1¼ tablespoon of olive oil plus 1 tablespoon butter.

Fry liver with onion lightly. Season with salt and pepper. Squirt on a little lemon juice. Do not overcook or the liver will be tough.

Baked Heart

Clean and remove tough valves and arteries from the heart. Boil until tender. Split heart open and fill with dressing. Put the rest of the dressing around the heart. If completely covered, the heart will be better. Bake about 30 minutes at 300 degrees or until dressing starts to brown. Try this dressing:
1 large onion, diced
1 cup celery, finely cut
½ cup butter
½ loaf dry bread, cubed
1 teaspoon salt
1/8 teaspoon pepper
1 teaspoon sage

Cover onion and celery with a little water and simmer until tender. Add butter and leave until melted. Mix bread cubes, salt, pepper and sage. Pour liquid over the bread and stir until moist.

Venison Au Vin

Serves 6
¼ pound salt pork
1 pound venison (stew meat)
½ teaspoon black pepper
1 teaspoon parsley flakes
2 medium onions, quartered
2 cups fresh mushrooms
1 cup white wine
½ cup red wine
½ teaspoon salt
1 small bay leaf
2 cups diced potatoes
3 cubed tomatoes

Fry cubed salt pork until crisp. Remove meat and drain. In the hot fat, brown cubed venison, rolled in flour. Put wine, salt and seasonings in a Dutch oven. Bring mixture to almost a boil, and put in the browned meat along with onions, potatoes, tomatoes, and mushrooms.

Bake in 350 degrees F oven for 3 hours. Check to make sure it does not go dry. Add more wine if it is.

Serve over wild rice, or mashed potatoes with a crisp green salad.

Venison Burgers

Any part of the animal may be chopped for burgers. Use the tougher parts—neck, breast and flank. If the meat is very lean, chop some suet in with it, or add sausage, 1 part to 3 parts venison, before cooking. Use as you would hamburger.

Heart O' Deer

The first night after the first day of deer season: Slice deer heart about 3/8 of an inch thick crosswise. Fry slowly in butter with onions. A little seasoning adds flavor. Fry until tender...cooking too long makes it rubbery.

When you have time: Marinate the heart slices for about an hour in:

1 cup red wine
2 tablespoons vinegar
1 teaspoon salt
1 small onion, diced
1 teaspoon prepared mustard
2 bay leaves

Dust in flour and fry 5 minutes in butter.

Meat Pie

shoulder, flank, shank, neck

Use equal parts diced vegetables and cooked meat. Add seasonings, and cover with left-over gravy which has been thinned with water. If there is not enough gravy, use a bouillon cube dissolved in water. Bake in a covered casserole in medium oven (375 degrees) for 1 hour. Just before serving time, remove lid and cover with a crust of mashed potatoes, pastry or baking powder biscuit. The vegetables may be cooked on the surface burner and the liquid in which they were cooked may be used in the gravy. When vegetables and meat are cooked add the topping at once and brown in hot (400 degree F) oven.

Season casserole with thyme, bay leaf, savory, or parsley—to your taste.

Venison Stew with Dumplings

3-4 pounds venison (shoulder, rump, round)
5 whole carrots
5 whole potatoes
5 whole onions
turnips, if you want
celery, if you want
salt, pepper
seasonings to taste

Dredge meat with flour, salt and pepper and brown in fat. Braise the meat for 2-3 hours over a very low heat. When the meat is tender, add vegetables and cook until vegetables are done. 15 minutes before ready to serve, drop dumplings on top of vegetables. Cover and cook without removing the cover for 15 minutes. Make a gravy of the liquid in the pan and pour over the meat and vegetables. Serve immediately.

Venison Soup

2½ pounds venison (shank, flank, neck or breast)
2 quarts cold water
1 cup diced carrots
1½ cups diced potatoes
¾ cup diced celery
½ cup finely chopped onion
2 tablespoons finely chopped parsley
3 cups tomato juice
2 teaspoons salt
¼ teaspoon pepper
½ teaspoon savory
1 tablespoon sugar

Simmer meat in salted water for 2 to 2½ hours, skimming occasionally. Let broth stand overnight or until fat has congealed. Remove congealed fat and add vegetables, juice and seasonings. Simmer slowly for about two hours.

Venison Scrapple

2 pounds shoulder meat (pork, or venison, or half of each or veal may be used)
1 tablespoon salt
¼ teaspoon pepper
½ teaspoon sage
pinch of allspice
2 cups yellow corn meal

Cook 2 pounds shoulder meat until tender in 2 quarts of water. Remove bone and gristle and cut meat into cubes. Measure 3 cups cubed meat. Cool broth and skim off fat. Heat 5 cups broth and add 1 tablespoon salt, ¼ teaspoon pepper, ½ teaspoon sage, and pinch of allspice. Add 2 cups yellow corn meal and cook ½ hour in double boiler. Add meat, cook ½ hour longer. Pour into well-greased loaf pan. When cold, slice in ¼ inch slices, dip in flour and saute on both sides until brown.

Senator and Mrs. Kerry Kammer

Venison Scrapple

1 medium onion, chopped fine
small piece beef suet
2 pounds venison and bones
1 can sifted corn meal
1 teaspoon salt
little pepper

Brown onion in suet until delicately browned. To 2 quarts salted water add the onion, meat and bones. Cook until meat is tender. Cool, skim off fat and remove bones. Chop the meat finely. To the remaining liquid add enough water to make 1 quart. Add the corn meal, a few grains of pepper, the salt and the chopped meat. Cook 1 hour, stirring frequently to prevent lumping. Turn into a mold, cool, cut in slices and fry in pork fat until done.

Potato Sausage

4 pounds pork
8 pounds venison
2½ pails (10 quarts) potatoes
6 medium onions
1 cup salt
⅓ cup pepper
2 tablespoons sugar

Grind pork and venison as for hamburger. Peel and grind potatoes and onions (coarsely). Add salt, pepper and sugar. Mix together and put in casings that have been soaked in water for several hours or overnight. Put in casings as soon as potatoes are ground and mixed as potatoes will turn dark if let stand. Tie ends and prick each ring in several places with a large needle. Place rings in kettle of water. Bring just to boil and simmer for a few minutes. Boiling too hard can cause rings to burst. Cool, wrap and put in freezer. When ready to eat, finish cooking in a little water, simmering about 10 minutes or until done. This makes about 35 rings the size of a small ring of bologna.

Venison Mincemeat

2 pounds cooked venison, chopped in food grinder
4 pounds chopped apple
2 pounds raisins
4 cups brown sugar
¾ pound chopped suet or butter
½ pound currants
½ teaspoon cloves
1 teaspoon mace
½ teaspoon nutmeg
2 teaspoons salt
1½ teaspoon cinnamon
1 lemon, ground

Add cider to cover mixture. If cider is not available, use fruit juices or water with ½ cup vinegar. Sweet fruit juices reduce the amount of sugar required. Cook very slowly until the fruits are tender (about 1 hour). This will keep indefinitely if put in fruit jars.

Antelope Goulash

Very easy to do—uses tougher portions of antelope that are usually chopped into ground meat. Chuck portions are ideal.

2 pounds of small, white onions, sliced
8 oz. of fat (lard or vegetable shortening)
3 pounds stewing antelope, cubed
1 tablespoon marjoram
1½ tablespoon paprika
2 cans beef broth
noodles, if desired

Saute onion slices in fat until soft. Add cubed antelope and brown on all sides. Sprinkle marjoram and paprika over meat and cover with beef broth. Cover pot and simmer, slowly, 3 hours or until meat is tender, stirring often, and from time to time adding more warm beef broth. Gravy should be thickish. Broad noodles are excellent with this with the gravy liberally spooned over them. A fresh green vegetable is an eye-appealing accompaniment, along with a beverage.

Elk Summer Sausage

28 pounds elk
8 pounds pork
¼ pound freezem pickle
¼ cup black pepper
½ pound brown sugar
1 pound canning salt
1 oz. mustard seed
1 oz. whole black pepper (cracked in blender)

Cube meat—place in crock or crispers in refrigerator.

Mix all ingredients except mustard seed and whole pepper. Sprinkle over meat and mix. Cure for three days in refrigerator or a cool place before grinding. Grind with coarse plate, then add mustard and pepper and grind again using fine plate. Stuff into plastic casing, secure ends and smoke. This can be hot smoked at a locker plant, smoked at home, or liquid smoke can be added (very sparingly) just before grinding and oven smoked at 150° for 6 to 8 hours, depending on the size of casing used.

Do not use much pork fat. Trim the fat off and use lean side pork. This is a real meat "stretcher" for the thrifty and a good way to use up meat that is reaching a freezer-burned state.

Jim and Mary Dugan • Towner, N. Dakota

Venison Bourguignon

3 pounds venison, cut in 1 inch cubes
2 cups Red Burgundy wine
½ cup butter
2¼ cups mushroom caps
10 small onions, peeled
1 package Beef Stew Seasoning
1 package Brown Gravy mix
1 cup water
salt and pepper to taste
dash Worcestershire Sauce

Brown venison in butter; add gravy and beef stew seasoning mix, water and 1 cup Burgundy. Cover and place in 350 degrees F oven until almost tender. Add mushrooms, onions and 1 cup Burgundy. Cook until onions are tender. Serve over rice or noodles.
Tom Washington

Special Occasion Venison

Mix:
2 cups red wine
juice of 1 lime and 2 lemons
2 bay leaves (crushed)
2 cloves, bruised
1 clove garlic, mashed
2 stalks celery, chopped
6 slices onion
6 slices carrot
6 peppercorns
1 pinch thyme
½ teaspoon salt

Soak 3 pound piece of lean venison in this brew for an hour or so. Remove meat and cut into 1 inch cubes. Fry in butter until brown. Finally, set meat aflame with 2 tablespoons gin and keep hot.

In another pan, brown 3 tablespoons pork, cubed small. Add this to venison. Strain the marinade and pour enough of it over the meat to moisten. To the meat mix, add 1 cup mushroom buttons, 1 cup small white onions that have been parboiled and tenderized. Cover the whole deal tightly and simmer for 30 minutes.

In another pan, saute 6 chicken livers and add these to meat mixture. Serve hot, garnished with croutons that have been fried in butter.

Venison Chop Suey

Serves 6
1 pound venison, cubed
¼ cup butter
1 cup onion, chopped
2 cups celery, chopped
2 tablespoons molasses
2 tablespoons soy sauce
1 can bean sprouts
2 tablespoons cornstarch
rice or chow mein noodles

Cook venison in butter; do not brown. Add onions, celery, molasses and soy sauce. Cook 5 minutes. Drain bean sprouts. Reserve liquid. Add slowly to meat mixture. Cook until thickened. Add bean sprouts. Heat thoroughly. Serve over rice or chow mein noodles, if desired.

Corned Venison

20 pounds venison
1 cup brown sugar
2 tablespoons saltpeter
3 cups coarse salt

Dissolve saltpeter, brown sugar and salt in 4 cups hot water. Put in large crock, (no metal container). Add enough water to cover venison by 2-3 inches. Weight venison down with a plate and clean rock on top. Cure 10-14 days in a cool place. Rinse venison and put in large cooking pot and add the following:
1 tablespoon thyme
2 tablespoons salt
1 large onion
1 teaspoon paprika
4 bay leaves
⅓ tablespoon pepper

Water enough to keep meat covered. Cook at medium heat 3-4 hours, until tender. Serve hot or cold. Cut into meal-sized servings and freeze.
Mark Dilts • Outdoor Writer & Photographer

Barbecued Elk

4 cups shredded meat
¼ cup vinegar
1½ cups water
¼ cup sugar
4 teaspoons prepared mustard
1 cup ketchup
¼ cup butter
¼ teaspoon pepper
1 teaspoon salt
2 slices lemon
2 diced medium onions
3 tablespoons A-1 sauce

Cook meat (brown) and add water. Cook until it falls apart. Add sauce. Serve on hamburger buns.
Adele Cermak • Okemos

Moose Casserole

2 pounds moose meat cubed
flour, salt and pepper
1 can mushrooms
1 package dry onion soup mix
1 cup canned tomatoes or 2 fresh tomatoes

Dredge meat in flour and brown in 3 tablespoons hot butter or oil. When browned, place in casserole dish and add rest of ingredients. Cover and bake at 325 degrees F for 2 hours.

BEAR

Bear Steak

Marinate the steak overnight or for 24 hours in the refrigerator in a glass or ceramic container in the following marinade:
1 cup dry wine
1 cup vinegar
3 bay leaves (Vary spices to suit your taste)
2 whole cloves
1 teaspoon whole black pepper
1 large onion, sliced

Remove steak from marinade and wipe dry. Roll in flour and brown in small amount of fat. Pour over it the following mixture:
½ cup water
¼ teaspoon garlic salt
½ teaspoon thyme
1 onion, chopped
dash pepper

Bake for 1 to 1½ hours in 325 degrees F oven or prepared in a dutch oven outdoors or on the kitchen stove.

Good for any meat which is tough or gamey.

Catawba County Wildlife Club • J. Wilfong

Braised Bear Steak

flour
salt and pepper
thyme
bear steak, 3 inches thick

1 cup sliced onions
4 tablespoons bacon fat
1½ cups broth
1 cup red wine
2 tablespoons tomato paste

Pound flour and seasonings into the steak with the edge of a plate or a meat pounder. Brown onions in the bacon fat and add the meat. Brown well on all sides. Add part of the broth and wine and bring to a boil. Cook briskly for 5 minutes. Turn the steak, reduce the heat and cover the pan. Simmer for 1½ hours, adding more liquid if necessary.

When steak is tender, remove it to a hot platter. Add the tomato paste and additional liquid if needed to the pan juices to make a smooth sauce. Taste for seasoning and pour over the steak. Surround with boiled potatoes, garnish with parsley and serve with sauteed mushrooms.

Appalachian Bear Roast

Trim excess fat from roast. Parboil in water with 4 apples added to each quart of water. When apples start to fall apart remove the meat. Salt and pepper meat, and bake it in a roaster in 350 degree F. oven until tender.

Be sure meat is well done. Even when cooked it may have a pinkish tinge which will darken on contact with air.

Bear Roast

Season bear roast with onion, celery stalks, salt and garlic if you like. Bake for one hour per pound at 325°. The last half hour, add 3-4 slices of bacon over top of roast. The meat will have a slight pink cast when first cut and darkens when sliced and in contact with air. Cold bear roast makes good sandwiches.

Curried Bear Meat

Use leftover roast. Chop 2 medium onions and saute in ¼ pound oleo. Add 1 teaspoon curry powder and brown. Add cut up roast and continue to brown. Add 1 quart buttermilk and bring to a boil. Thicken with flour and add 2 cups hot diced potatoes. Serve over rice.

BEAVER
GROUNDHOG
MUSKRAT
OPOSSUM
PORCUPINE
RABBIT
RACCOON
SQUIRREL
WOODCHUCK

SMALL GAME

SKINNING. Small game—including beaver, muskrat, opossum, rabbit—should be skinned and cleaned as soon as possible after it is killed. If you plan to save the skin, be careful not to damage it. Cut off both hind legs, front legs and the tail, then cut the skin on the inside of the hind legs from the paws to the vent. Work the skin off inside out, being especially careful around the eyes and lips. Scrape off all flesh and fat, then roll the skin for later use.

Cut the head from the carcass. Insert your knife blade, sharp edge up, at the tip of the breastbone, then cut through the thin meat over the belly. Be careful not to puncture the entrails. Cut a circle around the vent and spread open the cavity. Take out the entrails by grasping above the stomach and pulling down and out from the body cavity. Take out the heart and lungs. Remove all musk glands.

AGING AND FREEZING. Most small game is better if aged 24 hours or more in brine to draw out the blood. Meat to be frozen should be cut into serving-size portions. Put two layers of wax paper between the pieces, then wrap them in airtight packages. Since small game contains more fat than large game, it will not keep in the freezer as long. Small game should be cooked within three months of freezing. See the FREEZER TIPS and FREEZER STORAGE sections in the "Big Game" chapter for further information.

BEAVER

A beaver gives a lot of meat, especially the older ones, although the younger, smaller ones are more tender. When skinning a beaver be sure to remove the musk glands on the inside of the legs and the castor gland under the belly near the tail. Then wash your knife carefully so none of the musk odor taints the meat. Beaver meat is dark red, tender, moist, and tastes like roast pork. Surface fat should be removed and the beaver cut in pieces and soaked in salt water with bay leaves and cloves. An old beaver will become more fibrous and stringy the longer it cooks. Try to prevent grease from accumulating in the pan.

The meat in the tail is tender and white. To remove the skin, broil the tail and the skin will blister off.

Roast Beaver Tail

Beaver tail is fat and juicy, contains a lot of meat which can be a delicious addition to bean dishes and pea soup, like pork.

Roast the tail in dry heat in the oven until the skin puffs and lifts away. Then it can be easily skinned off. Use the meat, then, to flavor other dishes.

Pickled Beaver Tail

Remove the tail (naturally!) Singe over an open flame until outer skin burls. Peel outer skin off and soak tail in salt water for 2-3 hours. Boil in salt water until tender. Marinate in vinegar, chill and slice. Serve as desired.

Mark Dilts • Outdoor Writer & Photographer

Roast Beaver

Serves 6-8 (depending on the beaver)
1 beaver carcass
2 small onions
bay leaves
allspice

Select young animal if possible, weighing 5-9 pounds, ready for the oven. Skin, dress, remove head, feet and tail. The animal must be handled so that no sand or dirt gets on the meat. The castors must be removed. It is usually possible to purchase properly dressed carcasses from a trapper or fur buyer when beaver trapping season is open.

Using a sharp knife, trim all fat from the carcass, down to the lean meat. Beaver fat, while not strong is too oily for the table. Salt and pepper and lay the entire carcass in a covered roaster, belly up. Put a small onion in the chest cavity and another between the hind legs. Scatter a few allspice and 3-4 bay leaves around on the meat, and roast, covered, as you would a turkey of the same size. Beaver is best well done, tender and ready to fall off the bones. Many rate it the finest of all wild meat.

Ben East • Outdoor Life

Fried Beaver

Use a small beaver cut into pieces. Remove fat and soak overnight in cold water, drain. Cook in small amount of water until tender, then fry with bacon and seasoning salt. Try some hickory-smoked seasoning salt on this.

Roast Beaver

1 small or medium-sized beaver
baking soda
sliced onions
bacon

Remove all surface fat. Cover meat with weak solution of soda and water. (1 teaspoon soda to 1 quart of water). Boil 10 minutes and drain. Cover beaver with bacon and onions and roast until tender. Tastes like roast goose. Use drippings in the pan to make gravy. Pour gravy over the steaming slices of beaver.

Beaver Burgers

Grind 2 pounds of fat, raw beaver
1 medium onion, chopped
1 small can tomato paste
1 cup dried bread crumbs
1 egg
salt, pepper
1 tablespoon Worcestershire sauce
1 tablespoon parsley
1 tablespoon brown sugar

Mix all of the above ingredients, form into patties. Broil over charcoal or under the broiler until barely pink in the middle. Set on toasted buns, cooked side down. Spread 2 thin slices of cheese across the top, criss-cross and broil again for about 4 minutes.

Sweet Pickled Beaver

1 beaver, skinned and cleaned
½ cup vinegar
1 tablespoon salt
2 teaspoons soda
½ cup dry white wine or apple juice
1 cup pineapple juice
juice and grated rind of one lemon
1 teaspoon cinnamon
½ teaspoon cloves
½ cup brown sugar
mixed pickle spices
2 tablespoons dry mustard

(1) Wash beaver thoroughly with salt water, then let soak overnight in enough cold water to cover, adding ½ cup vinegar and 1 tablespoon salt to the water.

(2) The next day, remove the beaver from the brine, wash and cover with a solution of 2 quarts water to 2 teaspoons soda. Bring to a boil, reduce heat and simmer 10 minutes.

(3) Drain and rinse the beaver, then place it in a clean pot. Add water just to cover. Sprinkle mixed pickling spice on top, bring to a boil, reduce heat and simmer 20 minutes.

(4) Drain and rinse beaver. Pat dry and place in roaster.

(5) Mix mustard, spices, sugar, wine and fruit juices and spread over beaver.

(6) Cover and roast 325° until tender, basting frequently.

Mrs. Carl Sisson • Hebo, Oregon

Beaver Tail Beans

Blister tail over fire until the skin loosens or dip the tail in boiling water for a couple of minutes. Pull skin off. Cut up and boil with a pot of beans. Add salt and pepper to taste. Some chopped onions add to the flavor.

Mrs. Carl Sisson • Hebo, Oregon

MUSKRAT
OR MARSH HARE

Muskrat meat tastes much like turkey. If you want to keep the pelt, skin the muskrat before dressing it. Remove the two musk glands at the base of the tail. Also remove the white stringy tissue from the inside of each leg.

Before cooking, remove all fat, both inside and out. Soak the carcass in a solution of cold water, salt, and soda overnight. The carcass may be salted all over lightly and placed on a screen or grill to drain. Pack it on ice for at least a day before cooking.

Muskrat Meat Loaf

Serves 6-8
1½ pounds ground muskrat
2 eggs, beaten
⅓ cup dry crumbs
1 cup evaporated milk
¼ onion, minced or grated
¼ teaspoon thyme
1 teaspoon salt
¼ teaspoon pepper
1 teaspoon Worcestershire sauce

Soak muskrat overnight in salted water (1 tablespoon salt to 1 quart water). Remove meat from bones and grind. Mix ground meat thoroughly with other ingredients. Place in meat loaf dish. Place dish in pan containing hot water. Bake in moderate oven, 350 degrees for 1¼ to 2 hours.

Ecorse Marsh Hare

6 muskrat carcasses
½ cup salt
⅓ cup black pepper
lots of onions
carrots, celery
apples
2 bay leaves
½ cup mixed spices
4-5 tablespoons butter

Boil all ingredients in large kettle of water until muskrats are tender. Remove meat and strain the broth. Let the muskrats cool. Fill an iron skillet with medium sliced onions, saute with butter and small amount of water to help steam. Salt and pepper the onions, add garlic pepper. Remove onions when they are tender and pour this mixture over the muskrats. Saute again, add a little more butter, and sprinkle with a little brown sugar. Serve piping hot with corn bread and currant jelly.

Michigan Special

1 muskrat
1 teaspoon salt
1/8 teaspoon pepper
½ medium sliced onion
½ cup fat
1 cup tomato catsup
½ teaspoon Worcestershire sauce

Soak muskrat overnight in salted water, (1 tablespoon salt to 1 quart water). Drain, disjoint and cut into desired pieces. Place in deep pan and add 1 quart water, 1 teaspoon salt, pepper, onion and cook about 1 hour. Melt fat in skillet and fry meat brown on one side; turn, and immediately pour the catsup and Worcestershire sauce over the meat. Almost cover with water (about 1 cup) and let simmer until gravy is thick enough to serve, about 30 minutes.

Batter-Fried Muskrat

1 large muskrat, in serving pieces
salt, pepper
1 small onion
½ teaspoon poultry seasoning
1 egg
1 bay leaf
1 cup pancake batter from mix
½ teaspoon thyme
1 teaspoon salt
shortening

Parboil muskrat in water to cover, salt, pepper, onion, poultry seasoning and bay leaf. Simmer until tender, about 1 hour. Lift out meat, pat dry.

Add seasonings to pancake batter and add to egg if the batter doesn't call for one. Dip pieces of meat in the batter and fry in hot shortening until crisp.

OPOSSUM

Cut the opossum from the throat to the crotch, and remove the entrails as soon as possible after killing to let the blood drain thoroughly. Carefully remove the musk glands from under the front legs and the small of the back.

Soak the carcass overnight in cold water with a tablespoon of salt and soda and a grated potato added. Young opossums are usually parboiled before roasting or frying. The meat is light-colored and very tender. Be sure to cut off most of the outside fat and keep grease from accumulating in the pan.

Roast Opossum

Serves 2-4
1 possum, ready to cook
salt, pepper
1 medium onion, diced
1 medium apple, diced
1 stalk celery, diced
4 strips bacon
1 cup seasoned bread cubes
1 egg, beaten

Rub opossum with salt and pepper. Cook bacon until crisp. Remove bacon, and cook onion and celery in the fat until tender. Add onions and celery and fat to bread crumbs, egg and seasonings and apple. Add water if not moist enough.

Stuff possum cavity loosely with dressing and skewer opening. Place belly down in roasting pan. Brush back with oil. Add water to pan, enough to come about half-way up sides of opossum. Roast in 350 degree oven until tender, basting every 15 minutes. Bake uncovered 2½ hours.

Opossum with Sassafras

Roast opossum is good when baked with sassafras twigs when that spicy bush is close by. Rub the meat with salt and pepper inside and out, and stick lots of sassafras twigs into the outside. Roast uncovered at 300 degrees, ½ hour for every pound of meat.

Opossum Pea Soup

1 possum breast and meaty legs
¼ pound diced salt pork
2 medium diced onions
1 pound split peas
1 carrot, chopped
½ teaspoon tarragon
salt, pepper

Soak peas overnight. Drain and cover with 2 quarts cold water. Add rest of ingredients and simmer for 1-1½ hours, until everything is tender. Serve hot with oyster crackers.

Sweet Potatoes and Opossum

Serves 3-4
1 cleaned opossum
salt, pepper
water
4 medium sweet potatoes or hubbard squash for 4
butter

Clean opossum with damp cloth. Rub inside and out with salt and pepper. Lay possum in roasting pan on his back. Baste with melted margarine or butter. Add ½ cup water and cover and bake at medium heat (350 degrees) for ¾-1 hour. Split peeled potatoes in half lengthwise, or cut up squash to potato size. Place around possum. Add water as needed. Bake for another 20 minutes, basting occasionally. Uncover and let them finish cooking until golden brown and tender.

Roast Opossum Supreme

1 large onion, finely chopped
opossum liver and heart
2 cups browned bread crumbs
bay leaf
small red pepper, chopped
hardboiled egg, finely chopped
salt and pepper
Worcestershire sauce
3-4 tablespoons water

Mix all ingredients, and stuff opossum with it. Sew up opening with large needle and coarse thread. Roast in oven roaster on wire rack at 350° until tender and richly brown.

PORCUPINE

Porcupines are vegetarians, and they sometimes taste of the food they have eaten, usually pine or aspen bark. The meat is tender and should be parboiled, especially in late winter or early spring when the tree taste is strongest. Porcupine is fatty but delicious. The excess fat can be made into an excellent shortening.

Porcupine Mulligan

5-6 pounds porcupine, trimmed of excess fat. Cut into serving pieces
2 cups water
1 cup tomatoes
¼ cup vinegar
¼ teaspoon garlic salt
2 bay leaves
2 teaspoons salt
¼ teaspoon black pepper
¼ teaspoon each ground cloves, nutmeg, allspice, paprika

Brown porky in hot shortening in Dutch oven. Add the rest of the ingredients. Simmer for 1½ hours, until meat is nearly tender. Add:
4 diced potatoes
4 sliced onions, ringed
4 stalks celery, diced
4 carrots, diced
Simmer another 20 minutes until potatoes are done. Season to taste.

Porcupine Marinade

Serves 4
1 porcupine in serving pieces
1 cup soy sauce
1 clove garlic, minced
¼ cup sherry
1½ tablespoon brown sugar

Marinate porcupine in marinade ingredients for 24 hours, turning occasionally. Take them out and pat dry. Place on a rack in a shallow pan and roast uncovered until tender, at 350 degrees F. Baste every 10 minutes with marinade.

Porcupine Liver

Porcupines have large livers that are said to be a gourmet delight. Fry ½ inch slices of liver in a frying pan with butter and lots of onions only minute on a side.

Or, when camping, wrap bacon slices around a piece of liver and grill over the coals of a fire for a few minutes.

RABBIT

Rabbit is one of the most popular small game animals. Its meat is white and tender, often compared to chicken. Young rabbits are the most tender and the best tasting; a young rabbit will have a narrow cleft in its lips and smooth, sharp claws. When skinning, be careful not to cut the pelt because flying hair sticks to the bare skin. A cloth dipped in scalding water will usually remove this hair.

Rabbit meat is often parasitic. The internal organs should not be eaten even by your pets because they are likely to be infected with parasites.

Rabbit meat should be hung in a cool place for at least eight days before it is cooked. The meat is not fatty so it should be cooked slowly and with plenty of moisture. Rabbit can be substituted for squirrel in any recipe.

Hunter's Rabbit

1 rabbit
1 cup olive or salad oil
1 clove garlic
1 cup all-purpose flour
2 tablespoons dry mustard
1 teaspoon curry powder
1 teaspoon powdered thyme
2 teaspoons salt
½ teaspoon pepper
1 cup light cream

Cut rabbit into serving pieces, brush all over with oil, and refrigerate overnight. Next day rub pieces with cut clove of garlic. Combine flour, salt, pepper and spices in a clean paper bag. Shake pieces of rabbit in bag until well-coated. Fry to a golden brown in oil, turning until crisp. Reduce heat to simmer, and pour cream over rabbit. Cover, simmer for 1 hour or until tender. Serve on a hot platter with cream sauce.

Fricassee Fried Rabbit

6 pieces of rabbit
flour seasoned with salt and pepper
4 tablespoons bacon fat or lard
1 cup or so milk

Shake pieces of rabbit in paper bag with flour, salt and pepper until lightly coated. Heat about 4 tablespoons of bacon fat or lard in heavy frying pan and lay in the coated rabbit pieces. Brown thoroughly on all sides, turning frequently. Take the pieces out and put them in an oven casserole. Stir what seasoned flour is left in the bag into the frying pan, and make milk gravy. Pour the gravy over the rabbit in the casserole, cover and put in slow oven (about 300 degrees) for 45 minutes or until rabbit is moist and tender and has taken up most of the milk. Make more milk gravy if you like and have mashed potatoes too.

Fried Wild Rabbit

Cut rabbit up and add to salted water containing onions. Boil 10-15 minutes. Drain, season and fry until tender. Remove rabbit from pan. Add flour and water to drippings and simmer until gravy is done.

Rabbit and Broccoli Casserole

Serves 3-4
1 large rabbit about 2 pounds
1 package frozen broccoli spears
1 can cream of chicken soup
1 cup grated cheddar cheese
salt and pepper

Simmer rabbit in a salted kettle of water with onion and carrot and celery, chopped, for 1-1½ hours, or until meat falls from the bones. Let rabbit cool, then bone it.

Place rabbit pieces in the bottom of a buttered casserole dish. Spread the thawed, drained spears of broccoli over the top. Pour the cream of chicken soup over the whole dish. Salt and pepper. Bake at 325 degrees for 1 hour. Take out and sprinkle cheese on the top. Return to oven until cheese is melted.

Rabbit Pie

Makes 2 pies
1 large rabbit
1 pound pork back bone
2 teaspoons salt
½ teaspoon pepper
1 medium onion
1 quart boiling water

Place all ingredients into pan—simmer until tender, about 1½ hours. Remove meat and when cool, bone meat and cut into ½ inch cubes. Press meat down in bowl. Add just enough broth in which the meat cooked to barely cover the meat.
Pastry:
3 cups self-rising flour
½ cup shortening
¾ cup milk (more or less)

Cut shortening into flour. Add milk gradually to make a stiff dough. Roll out ¼ of this on floured cloth. Fit into pie tin. Place ½ of the meat mixture in crust, roll out top crust. Cut several slits for steam to escape. Repeat for second pie. Place in 400 degree oven and bake until golden brown, about 30 minutes. Thicken remaining broth and serve over the pie wedges.

Catawba County Wildlife Club • Joan Wilfong

Braised Rabbit

Serves 4-5
1 (2½ pound) young rabbit, cut up
flour
2 teaspoons salt
¼ teaspoon pepper
6 tablespoons shortening
1 cup chicken broth
3 tablespoons lemon juice
6 tablespoons orange juice
1 small onion, chopped
dash ginger
1 cup sliced mushrooms

Dredge rabbit pieces with flour, seasoned with 1 teaspoon salt and 1/8 teaspoon pepper. Saute until well browned in the shortening. Drain off excess fat. Add chicken broth, lemon and orange juices, and onion. Season with 1 teaspoon salt, 1/8 teaspoon pepper, and ginger. Cover and simmer over low heat until tender, about 1 hour. Add mushrooms for the last 15 minutes of cooking. Thicken juices with a little of the seasoned flour mixed with a little water.

Brunswick Stew

2 pounds meat (disjointed rabbit, squirrels or partridges)
¼ cup oil
1 medium onion, chopped
1 diced lemon
1 cup tomatoes
1 cup lima beans
1 cup corn
salt, pepper

Brown meat in hot oil until brown, along with onions. Add 1 cup water and tomatoes and cover. Simmer until tender. Then add rest of vegetables and cook 10-15 minutes until done. Salt and pepper.

Dutch Oven Hare

10 servings
Two snowshoe hare
Flour
Evaporated milk
Butter or margarine
salt, pepper
Heavy iron skillet with cover

Disjoint hare, cutting rib cage off before cutting back in half. Wash well and season with salt and pepper to taste. Roll in flour and brown in hot skillet (380 degrees). Do not place butter in skillet until it is hot and you are ready to place meat in it.

After every piece is brown, dredge lightly with flour. Then pour evaporated milk over pieces and into bottom of skillet. Milk should cover bottom of pan. Place in oven preheated to 250 degrees and bake until tender in closed pan. Keep bottom of skillet covered with liquid by replenishing with water when needed. Meat should come off bones easily when hare is ready to serve. Baking time is about 1 to 1½ hours. Can be longer at lower heat.

Ken Peterson • Flint Journal

Fried Rabbit

Cut rabbits or squirrels into quarters or smaller pieces. Place pieces in a deep pot and cover with cool water to which ¼ cup of vinegar has been added. Bring to a boil and let boil for 5 minutes. Throw this water away. Start over—cover game with cool water and add 1-2 teaspoons of salt. Boil until almost tender. Remove pieces from water and dip in corn meal or flour. Fry them as you would chicken. Using the above boiling methods removes any strong, gamey taste.

Rabbit is also good French fried.

Hasenpfeffer

1 large rabbit, 3-4 pounds; soak in marinade 1-2 days, turning every 10 hours.
Marinade:
2 cups vinegar
1 cup claret
1 cup water
1 sliced onion, ringed
1 teaspoon rosemary
1 teaspoon salt
½ teaspoon pepper
1 teaspoon dry mustard
6 whole cloves
6 bay leaves

Take rabbit out and pat dry. Dredge in flour, with a little salt and pepper added. Brown in ½ cup hot fat. Put on absorbent paper to drain, then in a pot. Strain marinade through a sieve, add to rabbit, plus ½ cup claret. Bring to a boil, cover and simmer until tender, about 45 minutes. Season to taste. Make gravy from the drippings.

Serve with potato dumplings.

Belgian Jack Rabbit

Cut the rabbit in serving pieces and salt and pepper to taste. Roll in flour. Brown all sides of pieces in ½ cup butter. Remove meat from the pan and place in covered baking pan. In the melted butter, add ½ teaspoon of nutmeg, ½ teaspoon cinnamon, and 2 teaspoons horseradish and a dash of red pepper. Stir and pour on top of rabbit; add ½ cup of water. Bake 1 hour at 350 degrees or until tender. Make a gravy out of the drippings, to serve over rabbit.

Gypsy Rabbit Dinner

Can also be used for muskrat, wood-chuck, porcupine.

Skin and clean a 3 pound rabbit. Cut into pieces for serving. Place in a kettle with a bouquet garni composed of 1 large bay leaf, 3 sprigs of thyme and 2 whole cloves, tied together with kitchen thread. Also 5 medium-sized onions, minced, chicken fat the size of a small egg, 6 crushed peppercorns and salt to taste.

Cover with equal parts of water and red wine, bring to a rapid boil, lower the flame and let simmer very gently for 2½ hours without disturbing. Then, add 1½ cup of diced carrots, 12 small white onions, 12 small fresh mushroom caps, peeled and 18 small raw potato balls.

Continue cooking, covered, until vegetables are tender or about 25 minutes longer. Remove bouquet garni and thicken the mixture with 2 tablespoons kneaded butter. (Equal parts butter and flour kneaded together.) Adding 1 generous tablespoon finely minced parsley, continue simmering for 4-5 minutes, then bring to a full boil and add the following dumplings:

Sift together 1 cup flour, 2 teaspoons baking powder and 1 pinch salt. Then, add alternately 1 whole fresh egg, beaten until light and enough cold milk to make a stiff batter. Drop by small tablespoons atop the rabbit ragout and let rise. Then cover and cook for 12-15 minutes more. Serve generously.

Canned Rabbit or Squirrel

Soak the meat 1 hour in brine made by dissolving 1 tablespoon salt in 1 quart water. Rinse. Steam or boil rabbit or squirrel until about ⅔ done. Remove skin and bones. Pack meat into hot Ball jars, leaving 1'' head space. Add 1 teaspoon salt to each quart. Skim fat from broth. Reheat broth to boiling. Pour over rabbit leaving 1'' head space. Adjust caps. Process pints 1 hour and 30 minutes at 10 pounds pressure.

Rabbit, Squirrel or Pheasant

Cut up meat, roll in flour, salt and pepper. Brown in oil in fry pan. Add 1 can mushroom soup and cook on the stove till done about 30-40 minutes.

Adele Cermak • Okemos

French Rabbit Casserole

1 rabbit, in pieces
flour
fat or oil
2 chopped onions
¾ cup seedless raisins
1 tablespoon vinegar
salt and pepper

Dredge rabbit in flour and brown in hot shortening in a casserole until brown. Add some water and allow to simmer for ½ hour. Add chopped onions and raisins. Put in an oven at slow temperature and then add vinegar. Bake until done, then salt and pepper.

Rabbit with Dark Raisin Gravy

1-2 rabbits cut in quarters
½ cup vinegar
2 teaspoons salt
1 tablespoon minced onion flakes or 1 small onion, chopped
4 whole cloves
2 bay leaves
½ teaspoon allspice
(optional)
½ cup dark raisins
¼ cup brown sugar

Place rabbit pieces in deep pot and cover with cool water. Add ¼ cup of vinegar to water and bring to boil. Let boil for 5 minutes, then throw that water out. Again, cover rabbit with cool water and add ¼ cup vinegar, 2 teaspoons salt, onion, bay leaves, cloves and allspice. Cook until almost tender, and then add raisins and brown sugar. Continue cooking until rabbit is tender and done. Remove rabbit from pot and thicken liquid with a paste of flour and water. Replace rabbit in thickened gravy and heat just before serving.

Rabbit and Rice

Parboil cut up rabbit 1 hour or until tender. If pressure cooked—leaves all the vitamins and proteins in the meat—time rabbit for 15-17 minutes. Parsley may be added in both methods of parboiling. Cut rabbit into bite-size pieces. Brown rabbit in butter. Prepare brown rice, wild rice, or long grain rice. To browned rabbit add fresh or canned mushrooms to taste and brown. Make a cheese sauce by melting grated pasteurized processed cheese with milk. The amount you make will depend on the casserole size. Combine the meat, mushrooms, rice and cheese sauce. Season with seasoning salt and pepper.

Squirrel may be substituted for rabbit.

Jeannine Staneway

Rabbit Salad

Substitute rabbit for chicken, or, even better, substitute showshoe hare for chicken in chicken salad. Excellent!!!

Rabbit Stew

Serves 6
1 rabbit
3 tablespoons butter
1 teaspoon salt
1 cup potatoes, (cut like little
French Fries)
½ cup celery, in strips
½ cup carrots
1 sliced onion
2 cups broth, from rabbit
1 cup tomato sauce
½ cup chopped parsley
¼ cup flour
¼ cup cold water

Cover rabbit with salt water and stew until tender, drain and save broth. When cold, bone it and cut up meat coarsely. Melt butter in frying pan, add potatoes, celery, onion and carrots. Cover and cook 15 minutes. Then add broth and tomato sauce. Bring this vegetable mix to a boil and add meat, parsley and salt. Add thickening and let cook for another 15 minutes.

Flemish Rabbit

Saute rabbit in butter until browned. Add one can of beer with seasoned salt to taste, and 1 small onion. Simmer on low heat about one hour, or until tender, and broth is like syrup. Turn and coat each piece. Be careful not to let it scorch when it boils down. Remove rabbit. Add water and thickening to make gravy.

Old Rabbit, Old Duck, Old Deer or Old Anything

6 onions diced fine
1 clove garlic, diced fine
6 potatoes, cubed
6 tomatoes, cubed
2 bay leaves
marjoram
peppercorns
parsley

Put everthing in a pot with 1 pint white wine, ½ pint red wine, and 1 teaspoon salt. Cut meat into cubes 1'' to 2''. Roll in flour and fry in vegetable oil until brown. Put browned meat with wine, vegetables, spice mix and simmer 3-3½ hours.

Remove spice bag and serve over rice, preferably brown rice, or wild rice.

RACCOON

Raccoon must be bled quickly and thoroughly after killing to keep the meat from becoming gamey. Skin before dressing if you want to keep the pelt. When the skin is part way off the front legs, remove the pear-shaped musk glands under each foreleg. Wash your knife and hands so the meat doesn't pick up the musk flavor. Remove all fat, inside and out.

Soak the raccoon carcass in a solution of cold water, salt, and soda overnight. Pack the meat on ice for at least a day before cooking. The meat is dark and sweet. It can be prepared the same way as rabbit.

Raccoon Fricassee

Cut raccoon in serving pieces. Dredge in flour seasoned with salt and pepper. Fry in hot fat until brown all over. Add 1½ cups water, ½ cup vinegar, 1 medium onion sliced and separated in rings, and 1 bay leaf. Cover and simmer for 2 hours, or until tender.

Take the meat out and thicken juice with flour and water for gravy. Serve raccoon and gravy with cornbread.

Roasted Raccoon

Soak pieces of raccoon in salted water overnight. Rinse off, dry and dredge in flour seasoned with salt and pepper. Brown in skillet in hot fat. Put meat in roaster, laying bacon strips over the top, until it is almost covered. Roast at 350 degrees F for 3 hours, or until tender.

Barbecued Raccoon

Cut cleaned raccoon into serving pieces, place in a pressure cooker and cook at 15 pounds pressure for 30 minutes. Place meat in a baking dish and pour barbecue sauce over it. Put in the oven for 1 hour at 325 degrees F.

Barbecue Sauce:
¼ cup vinegar
1½ cup water
¼ cup sugar
4 teaspoons prepared mustard
1 cup ketchup
¼ teaspoon pepper
¼ cup butter
1 teaspoon salt
2 slices lemon
2 diced medium onions
3 tablespoons A-1 Sauce

Put all ingredients together and simmer over low heat 15-20 minutes.

Raccoon with Sauerkraut

1 cleaned coon, in serving pieces
1 pound sauerkraut
1 medium apple, diced
salt, pepper
1 medium onion, diced
1 tablespoon caraway seeds
1 can beer

Dredge raccoon in flour, salt and pepper. Brown in hot fat. Meanwhile, stir apples and onions in 2 tablespoons fat until tender. Drain 1 can sauerkraut thoroughly. Add to the apples and onions, along with caraway and enough beer for sauerkraut to simmer. When it is heated through, put a layer in a roasting pan. Add raccoon pieces and top with rest of the kraut. Bake in 350 degrees F oven about 3 hours or until tender. Add more beer if it starts to dry out.

Stuffed Baked Raccoon

1 cleaned raccoon, parboiled until tender with salt, carrots, celery and onion. Bone raccoon. Make bread stuffing, from:

1 medium onion, diced
2 stalks celery, chopped
2 tablespoons chopped parsley
1½ large loaves of dry bread, cubed
sage, poultry seasoning
1 can cream of chicken soup

Mix stuffing together, adding water in which raccoon was boiled until dressing is moist. Put half in the bottom of a roaster. Spread the raccoon meat over the dressing. Cover with the rest of the stuffing. Bake in a medium oven, 375 degrees F, for 40 minutes. Be sure to add more water if it begins to dry out. Add 1 cup grated colby cheese to top of casserole, and put back in the oven for 10 minutes until cheese is melted and dressing is brown.

Cornbread Stuffed Raccoon

Rub whole raccoon with salt and pepper. Stuff with Cornbread Stuffing (below). Bake at 375 degrees F for 2-3 hours, depending on size and age of raccoon.

Cornbread Stuffing:
3 cups crumbled, stale cornbread
1 medium onion, chopped
salt, pepper
milk to moisten
½ cup celery, diced
½ cup corn
2 tablespoons butter or margarine

Melt margarine in pan, cook onion and celery until soft. If using frozen corn, simmer in water until soft. Combine all ingredients, salt and pepper to taste and moisten with milk. Pack into raccoon loosely.

Coon and Sweet Potatoes

2 large raccoons
1 ounce pickle spices (mixed)
½ pound brown sugar
sweet potatoes
salt
water

Cut raccoon into serving pieces and soak in salt water overnight. Parboil in salt water, changing water several times. When partly done, place in large roaster. On first layer sprinkle mixed pickle spice and brown sugar. Follow with layer of coon, spices and sugar. Bake in slow oven until tender and brown, turning and basting while baking. For the last 45 minutes put peeled sweet potatoes over top and finish baking.

SQUIRREL

The same process in bleeding and dressing as is used for other small game should be followed for squirrel. Gray squirrel is considered better than red squirrel in flavor. The carcass should be cut up, washed out, and soaked for several hours in salt water below 40°F. Like rabbit, squirrel doesn't have much fat, so it should be cooked slowly and with moisture. Sour cream complements the flavor of squirrel meat.

Squirrel in Sour Cream

Serves 6-8
4-6 squirrels, in serving pieces
salt, pepper
flour
1 cup sour cream
½ cup chopped onion
small can mushrooms
1 teaspoon paprika
shortening

Dredge squirrel in flour seasoned with salt and pepper. Brown them in hot fat in the skillet. Put meat in a casserole dish or roaster. Cover with sour cream mixed with mushrooms. Sprinkle top with paprika. Bake at 350 degrees F until done; about 1 hour.

Roast Squirrel

Young squirrel is tender, juicy and flavorful enough that it doesn't need the addition of spices and sauces. If you have a rotisserie, roast the squirrels while basting frequently with butter or margarine. If you want to roast them in the oven, put the young squirrels in an uncovered pan and bake in a slow oven, basting with melted butter or margarine, until fork tender.

Roast Squirrel with Sausage Stuffing

Serves 4-6
4 squirrels
1 pound pork sausage
1 medium onion, chopped
¼ teaspoon garlic salt
1½ cup cubed bread
½ teaspoon salt
½ teaspoon sage

Cook sausage in fry pan. Add celery, onion, and garlic salt and sage. Cook till celery is tender. Drain off fat. Mix with rest of ingredients and stuff into squirrel cavity loosely. Skewer or sew up the squirrel opening and place on a rack in roaster. Bake uncovered, at 350 degrees F, basting frequently till tender.

Squirrel for Two

Serves 2
2 squirrels cut in serving pieces
4 tablespoons butter
salt, pepper
½ teaspoon rosemary
1 bay leaf
1 cup small pearl onions
1 tablespoon chopped parsley
½ teaspoon poultry seasoning
1 cup dry white wine
1 cup hot water, in which is dissolved 1 chicken bouillon cube
2 cups sliced fresh mushrooms
2 cups cooked brown rice

Saute squirrel in butter and oil until lightly browned; add salt and pepper to taste, seasonings, wine and bouillon, simmer until nearly done. Add onions, cook 10 minutes. Add parsley and mushrooms, and cook 5 more minutes.

Serve with brown rice or wild rice and a crisp green salad.

Squirrel Barley Casserole

Parboil squirrel and cut in bite size pieces—brown.
Prepare barley:
1 cup barley
1 large onion
¼ cup butter

Brown barley and onion. Add 1 can of mushrooms and 3 cans chicken broth. Cook on low heat 40-45 minutes or until barley has absorbed all of the broth. Add barley to squirrel. Add one can of either mushroom soup or cheddar cheese soup. Heat squirrel, barley and soup and serve. Rabbit may be substituted for squirrel.

Jeannine Staneway • Lansing

Squirrel Hash

1½ cup diced cooked squirrel
¼ stick of butter or margarine
2 cups chopped boiled potatoes
½ cup chicken bouillon
1 tablespoon minced onion
½ teaspoon sage
2 eggs

Mix everything together but eggs. Salt and pepper to taste. Pre-heat oven to 350 degrees F. Make 2 shallow depressions in hash on top. Break eggs one at a time onto the top of the hash, being careful not to break the yolks. Bake in the oven until eggs are done and hash is heated through.

Brunswick Squirrel Stew

2-3 squirrels
1 quart can tomatoes
1 pint can butter or lima beans
1 pint can of green corn
6 potatoes, parboiled and sliced
½ pound butter
½ pound fat salt pork
1 teaspoon black pepper
½ teaspoon cayenne
1 tablespoon salt
2 tablespoons white sugar
1 small onion, minced

Soak the squirrels ½ hour in cold, salted water. Add the salt to 1 gallon of water

and boil 5 minutes. Then put in the onion, beans, corn, pork (cut into fine strips) potatoes, pepper and cut up squirrels.

Cover closely and stew very slowly 2½ hours, stirring frequently to prevent burning. Add the tomatoes and sugar and stew 1 hour longer. Then add the butter, cut into bits and size of a walnut and rolled first in flour. Boil 10 minutes and serve at once.

This can be used with muskrat, woodchuck, and porcupine.

Squirrel and Dumplings

Cover squirrel with flour, salt and pepper. Brown in deep fat for ½ hour. Put squirrel in a roaster and add garlic. Brown onions in the skillet you browned the squirrel in. Make a gravy, put it in the roaster, add water, and simmer for 2 or 3 hours or until squirrel is tender. Take squirrel from gravy broth. Mix thoroughly with a fork: 2 cups Bisquick and ¾ cup milk. Drop by spoonfuls in boiling gravy. Cook 10 minutes covered and 10 minutes uncovered.

Squirrel and Sauerkraut

Cut squirrel into serving pieces, season and brown in hot fat. Put in pressure cooker and cover with one can of sauerkraut. Add ½ cup water and cook for 20 minutes. This is also delicious with rabbit or chicken.

WOODCHUCK OR GROUNDHOG

Autumn is the best time of year to eat woodchuck. The meat is fine-grained and dark, and tastes like beaver. Bleed the woodchuck immediately after killing by cutting off its head. Cut off the three glands near the anus, being careful not to cut into the glands. Also remove the glands on the inside of the front legs and along the backbone. Trim away any excess fat.

Woodchuck may be soaked in cold water to which a cup of crushed spicewood twigs is added. The meat is usually parboiled before roasting or frying. Woodchuck can be cooked like rabbit, but take into account the fact that woodchuck is not quite as tender.

Woodchuck Patties

Remove glands from under forelegs and small of back. Cut the meat off the bones

and grind in a food chopper. Add salt, pepper, sage, diced onion, egg, breadcrumbs and diced salt pork. Mix thoroughly, form into patties. Dip patties into beaten egg and then into cornmeal. Wrap each patty in one slice bacon and skewer with a toothpick. Bake in slow oven for 1 hour.

Sunday Woodchuck

1 tender, young woodchuck, cut into pieces
1 can tomatoes
1 small can mushroom pieces
1 medium onion, chopped
1 bay leaf
salt and pepper
¼ cup flour

Dredge woodchuck in flour seasoned with salt and pepper. Brown in hot fat. Add tomatoes, onions, bay leaf. Cover and simmer about 1-1½ hours, until almost done. Add mushrooms and juice and cook until all are tender. Adjust seasoning.

Serve with boiled parsley—buttered potatoes and carrots.

Woodchuck 'Kabobs

2 pounds cubed young woodchuck
½ pound cubed ham

4 tomaotes, cut in wedges
2 onions, quartered
mushroom caps
large cubes green pepper

Marinate the above ingredients for 6-8 hours in earthenware or glass bowl, in following marinade:
½ cup olive oil
1 mashed clove garlic
¼ cup lemon juice
1 teaspoon onion salt
¼ teaspoon black pepper
2 tablespoons fresh chopped parsley.

Stir the marinating vegetables and meat once an hour to mix thoroughly.

Skewer meat and vegetables alternately on green stick or metal skewers. Broil over charcoal or wood coals until a chunk of meat is tender.

Gaylord-Style Groundhog

Cut the groundhog into serving-size pieces. Roll them in flour seasoned with salt and pepper. Put enough shortening in the pan to grease it. Brown the meat in the oven. Mince one clove garlic, and add it to the browned groundhog. Cover with water and simmer slowly until water boils away, leaving the meat a delicious brown.

BASS
BLUEGILL
BUFFALOFISH
BURBOT
CARP
CATFISH
HERRING
PICKEREL
PIKE
SALMON
SMELT
SUCKER
TROUT
WHITEFISH

FISH

Fish and shellfish are a complete protein food. They are also easily digested, rich in vitamins and minerals, and lower in calories than most protein sources.

Fish should be kept cool after it is caught to preserve the quality and flavor of the flesh. Clean and freeze fish or pack it on ice as soon as possible after catching it. If you can't freeze it immediately, keep it on a stringer in the water, then carry it wrapped in wet newspaper or burlap. Keep it out of the sun.

Another way to care for fish is to slit it open from the vent to the gills along the center line of the body, as soon as you catch it. Remove the gill attachment from the head along with the entrails. Wash and wrap the fish, then store it in a container with several holes for air circulation.

CUTS OF FISH

"Whole" or "round" fish is fish just out of the water. It must be scaled and eviscerated before cooking. Usually the head, tail, scales and fins are removed.

"Drawn" fish has had its entrails removed. Before cooking, its head, scales and fins should also be removed.

"Dressed" or "pan-dressed" fish has been eviscerated and scaled, but its head, tail, and fins must still be removed.

"Steaks" are cross sections of a dressed fish.

"Fillets" are the sides of fish, cut lengthwise away from the backbone.

CLEANING AND DRESSING FISH

SCALING—Wash the fish. Place the fish on a cutting board and with one hand hold the fish firmly by the head. Holding a knife almost vertical, scrape off the scales, starting at the tail and scraping toward the head (fig. 1). Be sure to remove all the scales around the fins and head.

CLEANING—With a sharp knife cut the entire length of the belly from the vent to the head. Remove the intestines. Next, cut around the pelvic fins and remove them (fig.2).

REMOVING THE HEAD AND TAIL—Remove the head and the pectoral fins by cutting just back of the collarbone. If the backbone is large, cut down to it on each side of the fish (fig. 3). Then place the fish on the edge of the cutting board so that the head hangs over and snap the backbone by bending the head down (fig. 4). Cut any remaining flesh that holds the head to the body. Cut off the tail.

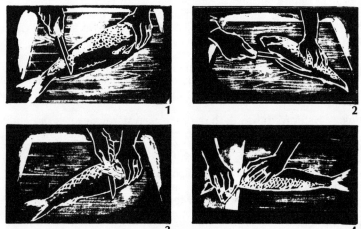

5   6

7   8   9

REMOVING THE FINS—Next remove the dorsal fin, the large fin on the back of the fish, by cutting along each side of the fin (fig. 5). Then give a quick pull forward toward head and remove the fin with the root bones attached (fig. 5). Remove the ventral fin in the same way. Never trim the fins off with shears or a knife because the root bones at the base of the fins will be left in the fish. Wash the fish thoroughly in cold running water. The fish is now dressed or pan-dressed, depending on its size.

CUTTING STEAKS—Large size dressed fish may be cut crosswise into steaks, about an inch thick (fig. 6).

FILLETING—With a sharp knife cut along the back of the fish from the tail to the head (fig. 7). Then cut down to the backbone just back of the collarbone. Turn the knife flat and cut the flesh away from the backbone and rib bones (fig. 8). Lift off the whole side of the fish or fillet in one piece (fig. 9). Turn the fish over and cut the fillet from the other side.

STORAGE

To reduce "fishy" odor or flavor, rub the inside of the fish with lemon juice (½ lemon per pound of fish) before storing.

Fresh fish should not be kept in the refrigerator more than two days.

See the FREEZER TIPS and FREEZER STORAGE sections in the "Big Game" chapter for information on freezing fish.

Fish should always be cleaned before freezing.

Frozen fish should be used within six months. An excellent way to freeze fish is to glaze them. Dip frozen fish in ice water, then freeze; repeat several times to build up a 1/8'' to ¼'' glaze. Wrap the fish in foil, plastic wrap or bag, and freeze. The glaze must be renewed every month.

Evaporation of water from fish flesh during frozen storage causes dry and tough fish. This is known as freezer burn. To prevent freezer burn, use aluminum foil or polyvinylidene chloride "cling wrap" to wrap fish. Polyethylene bags, freezer wrap papers, and boxes encourage freezer burn.

Thaw fish in the refrigerator, and use it soon after thawing. You may cook frozen fish without thawing if you add about a quarter more cooking time, but the fish will lose its firm texture. To fry frozen fish, fry at a low temperature until fish is thawed, then fry at a normal temperature only about half the time you would fry a thawed fish.

STORAGE LIFE OF FROZEN FISH AT 0°F.

Type	Species	Months
Fat Fish	Butterfish, Mackerel, Salmon, Shad, Trout, Whitefish, Tuna	3
Lean Fish (less than 5% fat)	Cod, Carp, Flounder, Haddock, Halibut, Lake Herring, Pollock, Whiting	6
Shellfish (all are lean)	Lobster and crab meat	2
	Shrimp	6
	Oysters, Scallops, Clams	3-4

COOKING TIPS

Fish have delicate flesh; cooking it too long or at too high temperature makes it tough and rubbery. To preserve its flavor and keep it moist, heat it only until the flesh becomes opaque and flakes easily.

The secret of deliciously browned, pan-broiled fish is dry heat. Use very little fat in the pan.

Whitefish, salmon and trout are fat fish, and the fat should be poured from the pan as it accumulates. Less fatty fish may be improved by basting with melted fat or a sauce.

Fat tissues should be cut out because they contain pesticide residue and off flavors.

One serving of fish is one-third to one-half a pound of edible fish. For whole fish, allow one pound per person. For a dressed fish allow half a pound per person. For steaks and fillets, cook one third of a pound per person. Leaving the skin on (removing the scales, of course) keeps fish juicier and more flavorful. Much of the "muddy" flavor can be removed by skinning the fish.

HOW TO SMOKE FISH

Fish flesh begins deteriorating as soon as the fish leaves the water, so it's necessary to take steps to preserve it by freezing, pickling, or smoking. Carp, suckers, buffalofish, catfish, salmon, trout and chubs are all delicious when smoked. Although whole fish can be smoked, fillets, chunks or pieces are easier to handle and permit more uniform salt and smoke penetration. Fillets should not be skinned, and bones are not generally removed.

BRINING

Fish must be brined before smoking to preserve the flesh longer and to leach out any residual blood. A glass, plastic, or stainless steel container should be used to hold the brine. You'll need one quart of brine for every pound of fish to be smoked. Make a solution of 1½ cups salt per gallon of cold water. Place the fish in the brine and keep it in a refrigerator at 40°F for 16 hours. Or else use the short method: make a brine of 4 cups salt to each gallon of cold water, and soak fish for half an hour. After brining, the fish should be rinsed in slowly flowing cold water for 30 minutes. This removes excess salt and blood and firms the flesh prior to smoking.

After freshening, drain the excess water and place pieces of skin side down on screen racks to dry the surface. In the early stages of smoking, the flesh surface must be dried to form a "skin" or "pellicle." This seals the surface and prevents loss of natural juices during smoking. If a pellicle is not formed prior to smoking, milky-colored juices collect in pools on the surface. A properly formed pellicle gives a shiny, dry surface to the flesh. Fish pieces should be dried on screens at 90°F for an hour and should be moved occasionally during the drying period to prevent them from sticking to the screen. Drying time will vary with the humidity and the amount of air circulated over the pieces. Using a fan will speed up the process.

SMOKING

Here are directions for two simple smokers to make. The first is the metal drum smoker, made from a 50-gallon oil or alcohol drum. Cut out the top of the drum, using a chisel or a cutting torch. Reduce the diameter of the removed top by about 3 inches. Suspend this top by 3 brackets 13 inches from the top of the drum, to serve as a heat baffle. Next, cut out a section at the bottom side of the drum for a fire pit door, approximately 10'' x 8''. Lightweight sheet metal may be used for a door on a single hinge. Make a tray for holding the fish from heavy ½'' or ¼'' wire mesh. Suspend this tray from metal straps so that it is 6 inches from the top of the drum. A wood or metal cover may be used to hold smoke in the drum.

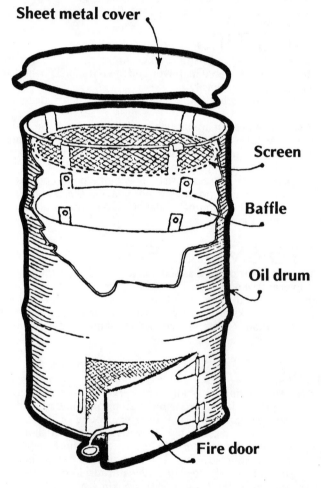

Sheet metal cover

Screen

Baffle

Oil drum

Fire door

METAL SMOKER

Another type of smoker is the wooden barrel smoker. Knock out the ends of a large barrel. Set it over a hole in the ground which is 2 feet deep and a little narrower in width than the diameter of the barrel. Nail wooden strips inside the barrel on two sides, a few inches below the top. The ends of the smokesticks rest on these strips. Place a loosely fitting cover on top. The barrel will not catch fire if ventilation is controlled and if fire is smothered to form smoke rather than flames. Keep door and top closed during smoking. Allow just enough air to enter to keep fire smoldering. Suspend some type of rods, iron or wooden, at the top of the barrel. Space far enough apart so fish do not touch when hung. A rack of coarse wire mesh may be used in place of rods. Make hooks of 8 or 10 gauge steel wire about 14 inches long or from coat hanger wires. Bend a loop in the center of the wire large enough to slide over the rods. Bend the ends of the wire in such a way that fish will not slip off during smoking. Place a wire mesh tray underneath the hanging fish to catch any that may fall off the rods during smoking.

WOOD BARREL SMOKER

Almost any non-resinous hard wood can be used for smoking. Hickory, apple, oak, maple, alder, beech, white birch, or ash chips or sawdust will give a good smoke. Different woods will give fish different flavors, so experiment to see which you like best. Kindle the fire, and get a good bed of coals before putting the fish inside. Stoke the fire every half hour or as needed, keeping it at a smolder with no flames.

Place the fish (skin side down if you're putting them on wire mesh) in the smoker when the air temperature reaches 100°F. A regular meat thermometer can be hung on a rack in the center of the smoker or inserted through a hole in the smoker cover to guide you on temperature. Another thermometer should be inserted in the thickest flesh section to keep track of the internal temperature. During the first two hours, cool smoke should be applied while the fish temperature does not exceed 95°F. This completes the pellicle formation and slowly develops brown coloring. After the initial two-hour period, the smoker temperature should be raised to about 225°F. A final internal flesh temperature of 180°F will be reached after three to four hours of this higher heat. Hold the fish at this temperature for 30 minutes to cook the fish and to inhibit bacteria from growing. As soon as the smoking is completed, wrap the fish in metal foil or wax paper, and store in a refrigerator or some other cool (40°F), dry, and insect-free place. If smoked fish is to be stored longer than several days, it should be wrapped in vapor-proof film or placed in an airtight container and frozen. Upon thawing, the wrapping should be removed and the fish should be consumed within a few days. Frozen smoked fish will keep safely for about one month.

HOW TO CAN FISH

There are many methods for canning fish. You must process fish in a pressure cooker to get high enough temperatures to prevent botulism. Start the timing process after the pressure reaches 10 pounds. If, at the end of the process, the jars have failed to seal, or you aren't sure if the proper time or temperature was used, refrigerate the fish immediately and consume it within 5 days, or freeze it.

The first way to can fish is to clean, wash and skin the fish. Cut it in pieces two to three inches long. Soak in salt water for 2 to 3 hours, then drain on absorbent paper. Pack the fish loosely in quart jars. To each jar, add two tablespoons of vinegar and one teaspoon salt, then fill the jar with tomato juice to within 1'' of the top. With a knife, work the juices around the side to remove any air pockets that have formed. Seal the jars and process in a pressure cooker at 10 pounds for 90-100 minutes.

A second method is to heat together a 14 oz. bottle of ketchup, a 14 oz. bottle of vinegar, 8 teaspoons salt, and a teaspoon onion salt (or one minced onion), and two bay leaves. Pour the mixture over fish pieces in pint jars, leaving one inch head space at the top of the jars. Process at 10 pounds pressure for 90 minutes. This will be enough liquid for 8 pints. You may wish to water down the vinegar with a little distilled or tap water for a less sharp taste.

A third method is to make a brine of one cup salt in one gallon of cool water. Cut fish into jar-length pieces. Soak them for one hour in canning jars, the skin side next to the glass, leaving an inch of head space. Put the open jars into a kettle. Cover them with hot brine (½ cup salt to each gallon of water) and boil for 15 minutes. Remove the jars and invert them to drain for five minutes. Put on caps and process for 100 minutes at 10 pounds pressure.

Fish Dinner

4 pounds fish fillets
1 cup flour
salt, pepper
1 cup thinly sliced onions
6 cups thinly sliced potatoes
1 can tomatoes (1 pound, 12 ounces)
¼ cup ketchup
1⅓ tablespoon salt
2 slices cheese, diced

Mix flour, 2 teaspoons salt and pepper, and roll fish in it. Fry fish in hot fat for 3-4 minutes or more until brown. Turn fish carefully. Fry 3-4 more minutes until brown. Spread onions over the fish. Cover onions with potatoes. Mix tomatoes, ketchup 1⅓ tablespoons salt and pepper. Pour tomato mixture over the potatoes. Sprinkle cheese on top. Cover and cook slowly (simmer) for 50-60 minutes, until potatoes are cooked.

Oven-Fried Fish

For lean fish:
2 pounds fish fillets
1 tablespoon salt
1 cup milk
1 cup dry breadcrumbs, toasted
¼ cup melted margarine

Put salt in milk, dip fish in the milk. Roll fish in toasted bread crumbs. Rub a cookie sheet well with fat. Put fish on cookie sheet skin side down. Pour ¼ cup fat over the fish. Bake for 10-20 minutes or until cooked. Test the fish with a fork.

Fish Chowder

2 pounds pan fish, cut into 1 inch square pieces
1 cup chopped onion
¼ cup melted fat
3 cups potatoes (cut into bite size pieces)
2 cups boiling water
1½ teaspoon salt
pepper to taste
3 cups milk
1 can cream style corn
(1 pound can)

Fry onion in fat until well cooked. Add potatoes, water, salt, pepper and fish. Cover and cook slowly (simmer) for 15-20 minutes or until potatoes are cooked. Add milk and corn, heat again.

New England Fish Chowder

Serves 6
1 pound fish fillets or steaks
2 tablespoons chopped bacon or salt pork
½ cup chopped onion
2½ cups diced potatoes
1½ cup boiling water
1 teaspoon salt

dash pepper
2 cups milk
1 tablespoon butter
chopped parsley

Remove skin and bones from fish. Cut fish into 1'' pieces. Fry bacon until crisp. Add onion and cook until tender. Add potatoes, water, seasonings and fish. Cover and simmer for 15-20 minutes or until potatoes are tender. Add milk and butter. Heat. Sprinkle with parsley.

U.S. Dept. Commerce

Oven-Fried Pan Dressed Fish

3 pounds pan-dressed fish
½ cup milk
2 teaspoons salt
1½ cup cereal crumbs or toasted dry bread crumbs
¼ cup melted fat or oil

Thaw frozen fish. Clean, wash and dry. Combine milk and salt. Dip fish in milk and roll in crumbs. Place fish in a single layer on a well-greased baking pan, 15 x 10 x 1''. Pour fat over fish. Bake in extremely hot oven, 500 degrees F for 15-20 minutes or until fish are brown and flake easily when tested with a fork.

U.S. Dept. Commerce

Beer-Fried Fish

3 tablespoons melted butter
¼ cup corn starch
¼ cup beer
⅓ cup flour
1 egg

Mix beer, butter, beaten egg yolk. Add flour and corn starch. Beat egg whites until peaks form and add to mixture. Use as batter for frying fish or chicken.

Fish Sticks

1 egg, well beaten
1 cup flour
1 cup cornmeal
salt and pepper
2 pounds fish

Remove bones from fish. Cut them crosswise 1½ to 2 inches thick. Mix all ingredients except egg. Dip each piece of fish first in egg, then in cornmeal mixture. Fry in shortening.

Fish Flakes

Eviscerate fish, and remove scales and gills. Cook fish in a covered saucepan with water, boiling slowly until flesh is tender and readily falls from the bones. Remove fish from water. Let cool and remove bones. Fish may also be steamed for 30 minutes in a pressure cooker at 20 pounds pressure, after which it is flaked by removing large bones. Use it to can or for fish dishes.

Pickled Fish

1 cup pickling salt
3 or 4 medium size sliced onions
3 teaspoons mixed pickling spices
3 bay leaves

Make a syrup of 1½ cups sugar and 4 cups white vinegar. Boil for 5 minutes. Soak 4 quarts of fish in salt water for 6 to 12 hours. Rinse fish 5 times or more in cold water. Cut fish in pieces. Put fish in jars, and add spices and onions. Pour hot syrup over fish. Cover jars with lids. Refrigerate for at least 3 days before sampling.

Meiken Ehlers • Harbor Haus Restaurant,
Copper Harbor, Mich.

Fish Casserole

1 medium onion
3 tablespoons butter
4 tablespoons flour
¾ teaspoon salt
2 cups milk
2 cups fish flakes
biscuits

Saute onion in butter. Blend in flour, salt. Remove from heat, and stir milk in gradually. Return to heat and bring to a boil, stirring constantly. Cook about 5 minutes. Stir in fish flakes. Pour mixture into well-greased baking dish. Place in 400 degree oven to heat while making biscuits. Place biscuits on hot mixture. Bake 20 to 30 minutes longer.

Fish Balls

Use 1 part fish to 2 parts raw potato. Peel and dice potatoes, and cut them into a kettle. Place fish on top. Cover with water and boil until potatoes are tender. Drain, and mash potatoes and fish together. Season with salt and pepper. Beat 1 egg. Add egg and 1 tablespoon butter to mixture. Mix well and shape into balls. Drop into hot fat and fry to a light brown.

Broiled Fish

Clean fish, and season with paprika, salt and pepper. Put fish on broiling rack. Cover fish with butter. Broil each side of fish 10 to 15 minutes, basting often with a mixture of butter, chopped parsley and lemon juice.

Low Calorie Stuffing for Fish

¾ cup chopped onion
1½ tablespoons butter, melted
2¼ cups chopped, peeled apple
⅓ cup chopped celery
⅓ cup chopped parsley
2 tablespoons lemon juice
¼ teaspoon salt
1/8 teaspoon thyme

Saute onion in butter. Mix all ingredients. Stuff your fish.

Schooner Steaks Flamingo

2 pounds fish steaks
2 teaspoons horseradish
1 teaspoon salt
2 tablespoons chili sauce
1 cup grated cheese
¼ cup melted butter or fat
1 tablespoon mustard

Cut steaks into serving-size portions. Sprinkle both sides with salt and pepper. Combine cheese, mustard, horseradish, and chili sauce. Place fish on greased broiler pan 2 inches from source of heat. Brush with butter and broil 5 to 8 minutes. Turn carefully and brush other side with butter and broil 5 to 8 minutes longer or until fish flakes easily when tested with a fork. Place cheese mixture on top of fish. Return to broiler until cheese melts and browns. Serves 6.

Fish Boil

Use a large kettle with a wire basket.
12 fish steaks or chunks, at least 1½ inches thick, about 8-10 ounces each (use whitefish, trout, salmon, halibut, haddock, pollock, red snapper, cod, king mackerel, grouper, seas bass, or rockfish).
12 to 15 scrubbed, medium sized red potatoes. Clip at the ends but do not peel.
12 medium onions, peeled
1 cup salt
optional seasonings—bay leaves, whole black pepper tied in cloth bag, drawn butter, parsley, lemon wedges

Place potatoes and 8 quarts water in kettle with vents open; bring to a boil. Add ½ cup salt and onions. Timing starts when water returns to boil. Cook for 20 minutes, regulating heat to produce a steady, roll action boil with cover vents still open. Place fish in basket and lower into water. Add seasonings in cloth bag and another ½ cup salt. Cover and bring to gently rolling boil for about 12 minutes. To test for doneness, spear potato with fork—it will penetrate easily if done. Fish is cooked when it flakes easily with a fork. Cooking time may vary a few minutes either way depending on size of potatoes and thickness of fish. Lift out basket with fish; drain water off potatoes and onions. Serve with drawn butter, parsley and lemon wedges.

Deep-Fried Fish

Fish should be filleted, boned and skinned. Fry one pound fish per person to be served. Cut fish into inch-square cubes. Salt and pepper, and roll fish in flour or seafood batter mixture. Fill electric fry pan with peanut or vegetable oil, and heat until temperature is 400 degrees. Use enough oil to cover fish completely. Fry to a deep golden brown, 8 to 10 minutes.

Baked Bass

2 pounds bass fillets
1 can cream of tomato soup
2 tablespoons chopped onion
¾ teaspoon salt
1 cup grated cheese
pepper to taste

Cut fillets into 6 servings. Rub baking dish with shortening. Put fish in baking dish. Mix onion soup, salt and pepper and spread over the fish. Sprinkle grated cheese on top. Bake at 350 degrees for 25 to 30 minutes, or until fish flakes easily with a fork.

Poached Bass with Egg Sauce

Serves 6
2 pounds pan dressed bass, or fillets
2 cups boiling water
¼ cup lemon juice
1 small onion, thinly sliced
1 teaspoon salt
3 peppercorns
2 sprigs parsley
1 bay leaf
egg sauce
paprika

Thaw frozen fish, remove skin and bones and cut fish into 6 portions. Place fish in a well-greased 10 inch fry pan. Add remaining ingredients. Cover and simmer for 5-10 minutes or until fish flakes easily when tested with a fork. Carefully remove fish to a hot platter. Pour egg sauce over the fish. Sprinkle with paprika.

Egg sauce:
¼ cup butter or margarine
2 tablespoons flour
¾ teaspoon powdered mustard
½ teaspoon salt
dash pepper
1¼ cup milk
2 hard cooked eggs, chopped
1 tablespoon chopped parsley

Melt butter. Stir in flour and seasonings. Add milk gradually and cook until thick and smooth, stirring constantly. Add eggs and parsley. Heat. Makes 1½ cups sauce.

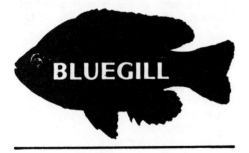

Deviled Bluegill

4 cups bluegill meat (drop fillets in boiling water, bring to boil again—remove and drain).
1 cup milk
¼ pound butter
1½ tablespoons grated onion
dash of pepper
3 tablespoons Worcestershire sauce
1 green pepper
4 thick slices white bread, crusts removed

3 tablespoons chopped parsley
¾ teaspoon salt
dash Tabasco sauce
1 teaspoon dry mustard
1 pimento, finely cut

Cook everything but the fish for 10 minutes, stirring. Then add the fish and cook five minutes. Put in a flat casserole and sprinkle crumbled corn flakes lightly over the top. Then brown in a hot oven (350°) 10 to 15 minutes. Serves six people.

Golden Puffs

¾ pound cooked flaked burbot fillet
3 teaspoons paprika
3 well-beaten egg yolks
few grains pepper
1½ cups mashed potatoes
¾ teaspoon salt
3 stiffly-beaten egg whites

Preheat deep fryer to 340°F. Mix together all ingredients except egg white. Then fold in beaten whites. Drop by teaspoon into deep fryer; cook until browned (3 to 5 minutes). Drain on paper towel. Serve hot, with lemon butter or tartar sauce. Serves 6.

Tangy Creole Merritt

3 cups hot boiled rice
4 stalks celery, chopped
1 tablespoon flour
2 teaspoons chili powder
2 cups cooked peas
1 tablespoon vinegar
2 cups cooked flaked burbot
2 sliced onions
2 tablespoons shortening or salad oil
1 teaspoon salt
¾ cup water
2 cups canned tomatoes (with liquid)
1 teaspoon sugar

Fry onions and celery in shortening until lightly browned. Add flour and mix until smooth. Gradually add salt, chili powder and water and cook for 15 minutes. Add tomatoes, peas, vinegar, sugar and fish. Cook until thoroughly reheated. Serve in a rice ring or on rice. Serves 8.

Harbor Beach Hash

3 cups deboned burbot simmered in water with celery tips and sliced lemon
6 small potatoes, cooked
salt and pepper
4-6 tablespoons shortening
3 carrots, cooked
1½ onions
1½ teaspoons dehydrated parsley flakes

Run fish, potatoes, carrots and onion through food chopper. Add parsley and mix well. Season to taste. Heat shortening in skillet. Add other ingredients and cook slowly, until heated thoroughly.

Sunshine Souffle' Lincoln

½ tablespoon butter or shortening
1 tablespoon minced parsley
1 small onion, finely chopped
1 teaspoon salt
1½ cups cooked flaked burbot
½ cup cooked rice
1 tablespoon flour
1 cup milk
4 tablespoons undiluted condensed tomato soup or tomato puree
3 well-beaten egg yolks
3 stiffly-beaten egg whites

Preheat oven to 350°F. Melt butter and blend with flour. Gradually, stirring constantly, add milk. Cook until sauce thickens. Add parsley and onion; cook a few minutes longer. Add tomato soup, salt, rice and fish. Carefully add egg yolks and egg whites. Place in greased baking dish. Set dish in pan of hot water. Bake 45 to 60 minutes or until mixture does not stick to a knife. Serve at once. Serves four.

Great Lakes Roll With Cheese Sauce

3 teaspoons chopped pimento
1 cup steamed flaked burbot
salt and pepper
3 teaspoons chopped green pepper
3 teaspoons chopped celery
Biscuit Dough:
¾ cup all purpose flour
1 teaspoon baking powder
5 tablespoons milk
½ teaspoon salt
2 tablespoons shortening
Sauce:
6 tablespoons butter or margarine
3 cups hot milk
6 tablespoons flour

¾ teaspoon salt
½ cup grated American or cheddar cheese

Preheat oven to 400°F. Blend fish, pimento, green pepper, and celery. Add enough cheese sauce to make mixture spreadable. Season to taste with salt and pepper. Cut shortening into dry ingredients for biscuit dough. Add milk, mix well, and knead on floured board. Roll biscuit dough into rectangle ¼ inch thick. Spread burbot mixture over dough. Roll up like a jelly roll. Place in greased tin and slash top. Bake 30 minutes or until done. Serve hot with cheese sauce. To prepare cheese sauce, melt butter in double boiler with flour, milk and salt. Stir until thickened. Add grated cheese. Serves 2.

Watertown Wharf Sandwich

¼ cup steamed flaked burbot
1 teaspoon chopped stuffed olives
2-3 tablespoons mayonnaise
2 slices bread
Swiss cheese slices
1 teaspoon grated onion
1 teaspoon chopped hard-cooked egg
salt and cayenne pepper
butter

Blend all ingredients. Season to taste; chill. Preheat broiler. Butter bread; cover with sliced cheese. Spread filling onto fish. Place on broiler pan 5 inches from heat. Broil until cheese is melted and fish browned; serve immediately. Serves 1.

Lakeland Cocktail

2 pounds burbot fillets
1 tablespoon salt
½ cup ketchup
1 quart water
½ tablespoon lemon juice
Sauce:
1 teaspoon prepared mustard
1 tablespoon Worcestershire sauce
1 tablespoon lemon juice

Simmer fillets in water seasoned with salt, lemon juice, and ketchup for 20 minutes. Cool, remove bones and break fillets into bite-sized pieces. Place on lettuce in cocktail glasses and chill. Serve with cocktail sauce. To prepare cocktail sauce, mix together all ingredients and chill. 6 to 8 servings

Buffalofish Chowder

Serves 6
1 pound buffalofish fillets or steaks
¼ cup chopped bacon or salt pork
½ cup chopped onions
2 cups boiling water
1 can (1 pound) tomatoes
1 cup diced potatoes
½ cup diced carrots
½ cup chopped celery
¼ cup ketchup
1 tablespoon Worcestershire sauce
1 teaspoon salt
¼ teaspoon pepper
1/8 teaspoon thyme
chopped parsley

Remove skin and bones from fish. Cut fish into 1 inch pieces. Fry bacon until crisp. Add onion and cook until tender. Add water, tomatoes, potatoes, carrots, celery, ketchup and seasonings. Cover and simmer for 40-45 minutes or until vegetables are tender. Add fish. Cover and simmer about 10 minutes longer or until fish flakes easily when tested with a fork. Sprinkle with parsley.

Sweet-Sour Carp

1 cup vinegar
1½ cup water
1 onion, sliced
1 lemon, sliced
12 raisins
6 whole cloves
bay leaf
2 pounds carp, filleted
salt
2 tablespoons brown sugar

Place the first seven ingredients in a sauce pan and bring to the boiling point. Add the salted fillets, cut into strips crosswise. Reduce the heat and simmer until the fish is done. Remove the fish and add the sugar to the liquid. When it boils, pour it over the fish. Chill and serve cold. This will keep 2 or 3 weeks in a cold place.

Escalloped Carp

2 cups cooked flaked carp
½ small onion, chopped
·3 tablespoons shortening
3 tablespoons flour
½ teaspoon paprika
1 teaspoon salt
2 cups milk
1 hard-cooked egg
¼ cup buttered crumbs

Cook the onion in the fat until tender. Add the flour, paprika and salt, then the milk, gradually, stirring until thickened. Place the fish and sliced egg in a greased casserole and pour the sauce over them. Cover with crumbs and bake in a moderate oven (350 degrees) about 20 minutes or until crumbs are browned.

Baked Stuffed Carp

2-3 pound carp, cleaned
salt
melted fat
2 bacon strips (optional)
stuffing
2 cups moist bread crumbs
3 tablespoons shortening
1 small onion, chopped fine
½ cup celery, diced
½ teaspoon thyme
1/8 teaspoon pepper
few spring parsley, chopped

Cook the onion and celery in the fat a few minutes. Add crumbs, seasonings, and parsley and mix thoroughly.

The fish may be whole or filleted, but the latter is recommended because the absence of large bones makes it easier to serve. Wash and dry the fish, and cut several crosswise gashes in the skin. Salt inside and out. Place the stuffing inside and sew or skewer the opening together. Brush with melted fat and place on a greased baking pan. Bacon strips placed on top of the fish will improve flavor and keep the skin moist. If bacon is not used, baste the fish with melted fat several times during baking. Bake in moderate oven (350 degrees) for 50-60 minutes.

Carp Flakes

4 pounds of whole, dressed carp
½ teaspoon salt
¼ teaspoon pepper
1 cup hot water

Cut fish into pieces for serving, and season each with salt and pepper. Place on rack in a covered pan containing water, and steam for about 10 minutes. Remove skin, separate flesh from bones, and flake with a fork. Yield: 5 cups flaked fish.

Carp Flake Loaf

2 cups cooked carp flakes
1 tablespoon lemon juice
¼ cup butter or other fat
¼ cup flour
1 cup milk
½ cup celery, finely chopped
½ cup bread crumbs
¾ teaspoon salt
1 tablespoon parsley, chopped
1 teaspoon onion, grated

Drain the fish flakes, and add the lemon juice. Melt the butter, stir in the flour and milk. Cook until smooth and thick, stirring constantly. Cool, and add all the other ingredients. Mix until well blended, pour on waxed paper, and shape into a loaf. Place in a shallow greased baking pan. Bake for about 45 minutes in a pre-heated oven at 350°.

Northport Poach

1 pound skinned carp fillets
2 teaspoons salt
dash nutmeg or mace
2 tablespoons melted butter
½ cup milk
1 small onion, chopped
¼ teaspoon pepper
1 well-beaten egg
¼ cup bread crumbs
Sauce:
2½ cups milk
4 tablespoons flour
2 tablespoons chopped parsley
3 tablespoons shortening
salt and pepper

Run fillet through food chopper 3 times. Soak crumbs in milk. Add onion, seasonings, egg, melted butter and crumbs. Shape into fish balls. Scald 2½ cups milk in double boiler. Add fish balls; cook 15 minutes. Serve warm.

To prepare sauce, melt shortening in sauce pan. Gradually, while stirring, add flour, and then hot milk. Season with salt and pepper. Pour sauce over fish balls and garnish with chopped parsley. Serves 6.

Missaukee Rice Loaf

3 cups cooked flaked carp
2 tablespoons grated onion
1 tablespoon minced parsley
1½ teaspoon salt
¼ cup milk
2 cups cooked rice
2 tablespoons melted butter
1 tablespoon lemon juice
few grains pepper
2 well-beaten eggs

Preheat oven to 350°F. Combine all ingredients. Place in greased loaf pan and bake 40 minutes.
Serves 6-8.

Oklahoma Fishwich

1 cup steamed flaked carp
½ cup milk
1 tablespoon melted butter or shortening
4 well-beaten eggs
1 tablespoon chopped onion
12 slices bread

Mix together fish, eggs, milk and onion, and pour into skillet with shortening. Cook slowly, stirring frequently, until firm. Serve between slices of buttered bread. Serves 6.

Island Fried Catfish

Serves 6
2 pounds skinned catfish fillets
¼ cup soy sauce
½ cup cornstarch
½ cup flour
Pineapple Sauce
1 tablespoon baking powder
1 teaspoon salt
¼ teaspoon pepper
1 cup water
1 egg, beaten

Cut fillets into strips, approximately 1 x 2''. Place fish in a shallow baking dish.

Pour soy sauce over fish. Let stand for 30 minutes, turning once. Sift dry ingredients together. Combine water and egg; blend into flour mixture. Dip fish into batter. Fry immediately in deep fat, 350 degrees F for 5-6 minutes or until brown and fish flakes easily when tested with a fork. Drain on absorbent paper. Keep warm. Pour pineapple sauce on a warm platter. Place fish on top.
Pineapple sauce:
1 can (1 pound 4½ ounce) pineapple tidbits
2 tablespoons cornstarch
¼ cup cold water
Heat pineapple and juice. Dissolve cornstarch in water. Add gradually to pineapple and cook until thickened, stirring constantly. Keep warm. Makes approximately 2 cups of sauce.

Fast Fish Broil

Serves 6
2 pounds skinless catfish fillets
¼ cup garlic French dressing
3 tablespoons soy sauce
¾ teaspoon ground ginger
lime slices
Place fillets in a single layer, skinned side down, on a bake and serve platter, 16 x 10 inches. Combine French dressing, soy sauce, ginger. Pour sauce over fillets and let stand 10 minutes. Broil about 4 inches from source of heat for 10-15 minutes or until fillets flake easily when tested with a fork. Baste once during broiling with sauce in pan. Garnish with lime slices.

Tennessee Fried Catfish

Serves 6
6 skinned, pan dressed catfish or other fish
2 teaspoons salt
¼ teaspoon pepper
2 eggs
2 tablespoons milk
2 cups cornmeal
Thaw frozen fish. Sprinkle both sides with salt and pepper. Beat eggs slightly and blend in milk. Dip fish in the eggs and roll in cornmeal. Place fish in a heavy fry pan which contains 1/8 inch of melted fat, hot but not smoking. Fry at moderate heat. When fish is brown on one side, turn carefully and brown the other side.

Cooking time is about 10 minutes, depending on the thickness of the fish. Drain on absorbent paper. Serve immediately on a hot platter, plain or with a sauce.

Smokey Broiled Catfish

Serves 6
6 skinned, pan dressed catfish
⅓ cup soy sauce
3 tablespoons melted fat or oil
1 tablespoon liquid smoke
1 clove garlic, finely chopped
½ teaspoon ginger
½ teaspoon salt
lemon wedges
Thaw frozen fish. Clean, wash and dry fish. Combine remaining ingredients except lemon wedges and mix thoroughly. Brush inside of fish with sauce. Place fish on a well-greased broiler pan, brush with sauce. Broil about 3 inches from source of heat for 4-6 minutes. Turn carefully and brush other side with sauce. Broil 4-6 minutes longer, basting occasionally, until fish flakes easily when tested with a fork. Serve with lemon wedges.

Catfish Gumbo

Serves 6
1 pound skinned catfish fillets
½ cup chopped celery
½ cup chopped green pepper
1 clove garlic, finely chopped
¼ cup melted fat or oil
2 beef bouillon cubes
2 cups boiling water
1 can (1 pound) tomatoes
1 package (10 oz.) frozen okra, sliced
2 teaspoons salt
¼ teaspoon pepper
¼ teaspoon thyme
1 whole bay leaf
dash liquid hot pepper sauce
1½ cups hot cooked rice
Cut thawed fillets into 1'' pieces. Cook celery, green pepper, onion, and garlic in fat until tender. Dissolve bouillon cubes in water. Add bouillon, tomatoes, okra and seasonings. Cover and simmer for 30 minutes. Add fish. Cover and simmer 15 minutes longer or until fish flakes easily when tested with a fork. Remove bay leaf. Place ¼ cup rice in each of 6 soup bowls. Fill with gumbo.

Zippy Broiled Catfish

Serves 6
6 skinned, pandressed catfish
4 tablespoons lemon juice
2 teaspoons salt
dash pepper
1 cup flour
1⅓ cup Italian salad dressing
lemon wedges
parsley

Thaw frozen fish. Clean, wash and dry fish. Brush inside of fish with lemon juice, sprinkle with salt and pepper. Roll fish in flour. Shake off excess flour. Place fish in a well-greased broiler pan. Brush with salad dressing. Broil about 4 inches from source of heat for 4-6 minutes, basting occasionally. Turn carefully and brush with salad dressing. Broil 4-6 minutes longer or until fish flakes easily when tested with a fork. Garnish with lemon wedges and parsley.

Dixieland Catfish

Serves 6
6 skinned, pan-dressed catfish
½ cup French dressing
12 thin lemon slices
paprika

Thaw frozen fish. Clean wash and dry fish. Brush inside and out with dressing. Cut 6 lemon slices in half. Place 2 halves in each body cavity. Place fish in well-greased baking dish, 14 x 9 x 2''. Place a lemon slice on each fish. Brush top of fish with remaining dressing. Sprinkle with paprika. Bake in moderate oven, 350 degrees F for 30-35 minutes or until fish flakes easily when tested with a fork.

New Orleans Catfish

Serves 6
2 pounds catfish steaks or other fish
½ teaspoon salt
dash pepper
2 cups cooked rice
¼ cup butter or margarine
2 tablespoons grated onion
½ teaspoon curry powder
6 thin lemon slices
chopped parsley

Thaw frozen steaks. Cut into serving size portions and place in well greased baking dish, 13 x 9 x 2''. Sprinkle fish with salt and pepper. Combine rice, onion and curry powder, spread over fish. Top with

lemon slices and dot with butter. Cover, bake 350 degrees F for 25-35 minutes, or until fish flakes easily when tested with a fork. Remove cover the last few minutes of cooking to allow for slight browning. Sprinkle with parsley.

Tangy Baked Lake Herring

Serves 6
6 pan-dressed lake herring or other small dressed fish
1 teaspoon salt
¼ teaspoon pepper
¼ cup butter or margarine, softened
paprika
2 tablespoons drained horseradish
2 teaspoons lemon juice
2 teaspoons prepared mustard
1 cup crushed potato chips

Clean, wash and dry fish. Sprinkle inside and out with salt and pepper. Combine butter, horseradish, lemon juice and mustard; mix thoroughly. Spread inside of each fish with approximately 1½ teaspoons seasoned butter. Place fish in a well-greased baking dish, 12 x 8 x 2''. Spread remaining butter over top of fish. Sprinkle with chips and paprika. Bake in a moderate oven, 350 degrees F for 25-30 minutes, or until fish flakes easily when tested with a fork.

Chipper Perch

Serves 6
2 pounds perch fillets
½ cup Caesar salad dressing
1 cup crushed potato chips
½ cup shredded sharp Cheddar cheese

Dip fillets in salad dressing. Place fillets in a single layer, skin side down, on a baking pan, 15 x 10 x 1''. Combine crushed chips and cheese. Sprinkle over fillets. Bake in an extremely hot oven, 500 degrees F, for 10-15 minutes or until fillets flake easily when tested with a fork.

Breakfast Perch

Serves 6
2 pounds perch fillets
¼ cup lemon juice
3 eggs, beaten
1½ teaspoon salt
1 cup flour

Place fish in shallow baking dish. Pour lemon juice over fish and let stand 10 minutes, turning once. Combine egg and salt. Roll fillets in flour and dip in egg. Fry immediately in hot fat at moderate heat until brown on one side. Turn carefully and brown on the other side. Cooking time approximately 6-8 minutes depending on thickness of fish.

Oven-Barbecued Perch

Serves 6
2 pounds perch or other firm fish fillets
½ cup cooking oil
1 teaspoon salt
dash pepper
1 clove garlic, minced
1 cup shredded Cheddar cheese
1 cup fine bread, cracker or cereal crumbs
1 cup commercial barbecue sauce

Cut fish into 6 serving portions. Combine oil, salt, pepper and garlic. Mix cheese and crumbs. Dip each piece of fish into oil; drain; roll in cheese crumb mixture. Arrange fish in well greased baking pan. Bake in hot oven, 450 degrees F, 7-10 minutes. Heat barbecue sauce. Spoon ½ of sauce over fish. Keep remaining sauce hot. Cook fish an additional 5 minutes or until it flakes easily. Serve with remaining sauce.

Fish may be served with sauce on large, buttered, toasted hamburger buns.

Baked Yellow Perch Supreme

Serves 6
2 pounds yellow perch fillets, fresh or frozen
½ cup flour
1 teaspoon salt
dash pepper
¼ cup roasted, diced almonds
1 teaspoon grated lemon rind
¼ cup lemon juice
¼ cup melted fat or oil
¼ cup chopped chives
lemon wedges
parsley

Cut fish into single fillets if necessary. Combine flour, salt and pepper. Roll fish in flour. Place fish skin side down in a well-greased shallow baking dish. Combine almonds, lemon rind, lemon juice and fat, mix well. Pour over fish. Bake in a moderate oven, 350 degrees F., for 25-30 minutes or until fish flakes easily when tested with a fork. Sprinkle chives over top of fish. Garnish with lemon wedges and parsley.

Yellow Perch Tempura

Serves 6
2 pounds yellow perch fillets
1 teaspoon salt
1 cup flour
½ teaspoon baking powder
½ teaspoon salt
dash garlic salt
1 egg, beaten
1 cup cold water

Thaw frozen fillets. Cut into single fillets if necessary. Sprinkle with salt. Sift together flour, baking powder, salt and garlic salt. Combine egg and water. Blend with flour mixture. Dip fish in batter. Fry in deep fat, 375 degrees F for 2-3 minutes or until fish is brown on the side. Turn carefully. Fry 2-3 minutes longer or until brown. Drain on absorbent paper. Garnish.

Yellow Perch Parmesan

Serves 6
2 pounds yellow perch fillets
½ cup salad oil
1 teaspoon salt
1 clove garlic, minced
1¼ cup grated Parmesan cheese
1 cup finely sifted bread crumbs

Cut fish into single fillets if necessary. Combine oil, salt and garlic. Place fish in oil mixture for 10 minutes. Remove from oil, drain and roll in grated cheese. Roll in bread crumbs and place in a single layer, skin side down, on a well greased cookie sheet 17 x 14''. Bake in oven 450 degrees F 12 minutes or until fish flakes easily when tested with a fork. Garnish.

Scalloped Fish and Potatoes

Serves 6
1½ pounds perch fillets
⅔ cup flour
2¼ teaspoons salt
1/8 teaspoon pepper
3 cups hot milk
6 cups thinly sliced raw potatoes
2 cups thinly sliced onions, separated
into rings
¼ cup butter or margarine
paprika

Cut fish crosswise into ½'' slices; set aside. Combine flour, 1¾ teaspoon salt, and pepper; mix well. Spread ⅓ of the potato slices and ½ of the onion and fish slices in layers over the bottom of a shallow, 3 quart casserole. Sprinkle ½ of the flour mix over the fish. Dot with ½ of butter or margarine. Repeat layers. Cover with remaining potato slices. Pour milk over potatoes; press potatoes into milk. Sprinkle with remaining ½ teaspoon salt and paprika. Cover casserole with aluminum foil, crimping foil securely to edges of casserole. Bake at 375 degrees 1 hour, or until potatoes are tender and fish flakes easily.

Perch German Potato Pancakes

1 pound ocean perch fillets or other fish
fillets, fresh or frozen
3 eggs, beaten
2 tablespoons flour
2 tablespoons grated onion
1 tablespoon chopped parsley
applesauce
2 teaspoons salt
dash nutmeg
dash pepper
2 cups finely grated raw potatoes

Thaw frozen fillets. Skin fillets and chop finely. Combine all ingredients except applesauce; mix thoroughly. Place a well-greased griddle or fry pan about 4 inches from hot coals and heat until fat is hot but not smoking. Drop ⅓ cup fish mixture on griddle and flatten slightly with spatula. Fry 3 to 4 minutes or until brown. Turn carefully and fry 3 to 4 minutes longer or until brown. Drain on absorbent paper. Keep warm. Serve with applesauce. Serves 6.

Perch 'Kabobs

2 pounds yellow perch fillets or other fish
fillets, fresh or frozen

⅓ cup French dressing
3 large, firm tomatoes
dash pepper
1 can (1 pound) whole potatoes, drained
1½ teaspoons salt
⅓ cup melted fat or oil

Thaw frozen fillets. Skin fillets and cut into strips approximately 1 inch wide by 4 inches long. Place fish in a shallow baking dish. Pour dressing over fish and let stand for 30 minutes. Wash tomatoes. Remove stem ends and cut into sixths. Remove fish, reserving dressing for basting. Roll fillets and place on skewers alternately with tomatoes and potatoes until skewers are filled. Place kabobs in well-greased hinged wire grills. Add salt, pepper, and remaining dressing to fat; mix thoroughly. Baste kabobs with seasoned fat. Cook about 4 inches from moderately hot coals for 4 to 6 minutes. Baste with sauce. Turn and cook for 4 to 6 minutes longer or until fish flakes easily when tested with a fork. Serves 6.

Baked Pickerel Supreme

Serves 6
2 pounds pickerel fillets
1½ teaspoons salt
¼ teaspoon pepper
2 cans (4 oz. each) sliced mushrooms,
drained
¼ cup chopped onion
2 tablespoons melted fat or oil
¼ cup grated cheese
½ cup chopped parsley
1 egg, beaten
1 tablespoon lemon juice
1½ cups soft bread crumbs
1 large tomato, cut into 6 slices
¼ teaspoon salt
dash pepper

Thaw frozen fish fillets. Skin fillets and cut into serving-size portions. Sprinkle both sides with salt and pepper. Place in a single layer in a well-greased baking dish, 12 x 8 x 2''. Cook mushrooms and onion in fat until tender, add parsley. Combine egg and lemon juice. Brush fish with egg mixture. Top with crumbs. Arrange tomatoes over crumbs; sprinkle with salt and pepper. Spread mushroom mixture over tomatoes; sprinkle with cheese. Bake in moderate oven, 350 degrees F for 30-40 minutes or until fish flakes easily when tested with a fork.

Crispy Walleye with Hot Chili Sauce

Serves 6
6 pan-dressed walleyes
1 egg, beaten
2 tablespoons milk
1 teaspoon salt
1 teaspoon chili powder
5-6 drops liquid hot sauce
½ cup cornmeal
½ cup flour
fat for frying
Hot chili sauce

Clean, wash and dry fish. Combine egg, milk, salt, chili powder and liquid hot pepper sauce; mix. Combine cornmeal and flour, mix. Dip fish into egg mixture, then roll in cornmeal mix. Place in single layer in hot fat in large fry pan. Fry at moderate heat about 5 minutes, turn carefully. Fry second side about 5 minutes or until fish are brown and flake easily when tested with a fork. Drain on paper toweling. Serve with hot chili sauce.

Hot Chili Sauce:
1 cup chopped onion
1 cup chopped green pepper
1 clove garlic, finely chopped
1 tablespoon shortening or oil
2 dashes hot sauce
1 can (8 oz.) tomato sauce
¼ cup ketchup
1 teaspoon chili powder
¼ teaspoon salt
¼ teaspoon pepper

Cook onion, green pepper and garlic in shortening or oil until onion is tender. Add tomato sauce, ketchup, chili powder, salt and pepper, and liquid hot pepper sauce. Cover and simmer 15-20 minutes or until flavors are blended.

Makes about 1¾ cups sauce.

Grilled Pike Fillets

2 pounds pike fillets
½ cup melted fat or oil
¼ cup lemon juice
2 teaspoons salt
½ teaspoon Worcestershire sauce
¼ teaspoon white pepper
dash Tabasco
paprika

Cut fish into serving-size portions. Combine remaining ingredients, except paprika. Place fish in well-greased, hinged wire grills (if cooking over charcoal). Put in broiler pan, if cooking indoors. Baste fish with sauce and sprinkle with paprika. Cook about 4 inches from moderately hot coals for 8 minutes. Baste with sauce and sprinkle with paprika. Turn and cook for 7-10 minutes longer or until fish flakes easily when tested with a fork.

Poached Salmon

Fillets or steaks.

Poaching liquid may be slightly salted water or water seasoned with vegetables and herbs, milk, etc. Bring to boil in shallow, wide pan. Fish can be poached directly in liquid, in cheese cloth or a colander. Place in single layers. Liquid should just cover. Simmer, uncovered, with liquid only trembling, until fish flakes easily. Usually takes 5-10 minutes. Can be done on top of stove or in 355 degree oven.

Poaching liquid may be boiled down and thickened for a sauce.

Broiled Salmon

Brush with melted butter. A little lemon juice gives flavor. You may want to add dill. Try a lemon butter sauce with dill which has been refrigerated several days.

Place salmon on greased broiler pan, skin side down, 4-6 inches from heat. Broil slowly. Fillets or steaks need not be turned if not too thick. Cook until flesh is delicately browned and flakes apart.

Baked Salmon

Season and brush salmon with melted fat, sprinkle with lemon juice. Place on greased pan. Slivers of garlic, herbs, etc. can be placed in fish cavity for seasoning if not stuffed.

Bake slowly in preheated oven 325 degrees to 350 degrees until fish breaks apart or flakes. Fish can be basted once or twice with melted fat, lemon juice, lemon butter, milk or cream. Flour or bread crumbs can be sprinkled over fillets or steaks.

Fish fillets or steaks can be partially covered at least for part of the cooking time, with aluminum foil to keep in moisture.

Bake about 8-10 minutes depending on thickness of the fillets or steaks, or until it flakes easily. Sprinkle with lemon juice. Serve with sauce.

Hearty Coho Salmon

Serves 6
2 pounds coho salmon steaks or other fish steaks, fresh or frozen
⅔ cup thinly sliced onion
1½ cups chopped fresh mushrooms
⅓ cup chopped tomato
¼ cup chopped green pepper
¼ cup chopped parsley
3 tablespoons chopped pimento
½ cup dry white wine
2 tablespoons lemon juice
1 teaspoon salt
¼ teaspoon dill weed
1/8 teaspoon pepper
lemon wedges

Thaw frozen steaks. Cut into serving-size greased baking dish, 12 x 8 x 2''. Place vegetables and spread on top of fish. Combine wine, lemon juice and seasonings. Pour over vegetables. Bake in moderate oven, 350 degrees F for 25-30 minutes or until fish flakes easily when tested with a fork. Serve with lemon wedges.

Baked Coho with Sour Cream Stuffing

Serves 6
3-4 pounds dressed coho or other dressed fish

1½ teaspoons salt
sour cream stuffing
2 tablespoons melted oil

Thaw frozen fish. Clean, wash and dry fish. Sprinkle inside with salt. Place fish on a well-greased bake and serve platter. Stuff fish loosely. Brush fish with fat. Bake in a moderate oven, 350 degrees for 45-60 minutes or until fish flakes easily when tested with a fork. Baste occasionally with fat.

Sour Cream Stuffing:
¾ cup chopped celery
½ cup chopped onion
¼ cup melted fat or oil
1 quart toasted bread cubes, or herb seasoned croutons
½ cup sour cream
¼ cup diced peeled lemon
2 tablespoons grated lemon rind
1 teaspoon salt
1 teaspoon paprika

Cook celery and onion in fat until tender. Combine all ingredients and mix thoroughly. Makes approximately 1 quart stuffing.

Oven Fried Coho Steaks

Serves 6
2 pounds coho steaks or other fish steaks
½ cup salad oil
2 tablespoons lemon juice
1 clove garlic, peeled and quartered
1 cup crushed herb-seasoned stuffing mix
½ cup grated Parmesan cheese
¼ cup chopped parsley
1 clove garlic finely chopped

Cut steaks into serving-size portions and place in a shallow baking dish. Combine oil, lemon juice and garlic. Pour sauce over fish and let stand for 30 minutes, turning once. Remove fish, reserving sauce for basting. Combine stuffing, cheese, parsley and garlic. Roll fish in crumb mixture. Place on a well-greased baking pan, 15 x 10 x 1''. Drizzle 2 tablespoons sauce over fish. Bake in an extremely hot oven (500 degrees) for 15-20 minutes or until fish flakes easily.

Full flavor of fish is retained by this quick-oven treatment. This method minimizes cooking odors, uses less fat and eliminates standing over a hot frying pan. This method gives a juicy, tender, nicely browned product—good for large groups.

Broiled Salmon Steaks with Herb Sauce

Serves 6
6 coho salmon steaks, ¾'', (about 2 pounds)
¼ cup butter or margarine
¼ cup dry white wine
1 tablespoon chopped parsley
¼ teaspoon finest herbs blend
1 clove garlic, sliced
1 teaspoon salt

Combine butter or margarine, wine, parsley, herbs and garlic; heat slowly until fat is melted. Let stand 15 minutes. Sprinkle steaks with salt. Place fish on well-greased broiler pan; brush with sauce. Broil about 3'' from heat source, 4-6 minutes. Turn carefully; brush with sauce. Broil 4-6 minutes longer or until fish flakes easily when tested with a fork.

Baste steaks with sauce several times while broiling.

Serve with lemon wedges.

Baked Coho Salmon Surprise

Serves 6
2 pounds coho fillets or other fish
½ cup thick French dressing
2 tablespoons lemon juice
¼ teaspoon salt
1 can (3½ ounce) French fried onions
¼ cup grated Parmesan cheese

Cut fish into serving-size pieces. Place fish in a shallow baking dish. Combine dressing, lemon juice and salt. Pour sauce over fish and let stand 30 minutes, turning once. Remove fish from sauce and place in a well-greased baking dish, 12 x 8 x 2''. Crush onions Add cheese and mix thoroughly. Sprinkle onion mixture over fish. Bake in a moderate oven, 350 degrees F for 25-30 minutes or until fish flakes easily when tested with a fork.

Baking tip: The most important principle to remember in fish cookery is not to overcook!

Gourmet Salmon Steaks

2 pounds salmon steaks or other fish steaks, fresh or frozen
1 cup dry vermouth
¾ cup melted fat or oil
⅓ cup lemon juice
2 tablespoons chopped chives
2 teaspoons salt

1/8 teaspoon liquid hot pepper sauce
1 clove garlic, finely chopped
¼ teaspoon marjoram
¼ teaspoon pepper
¼ teaspoon thyme
1/8 teaspoon sage

Thaw frozen steaks. Cut into serving-size portions and place in a single layer in a shallow baking dish. Combine remaining ingredients. Pour sauce over fish and let stand for 4 hours, turning occasionally. Remove fish, reserving sauce for basting. Place fish in well-greased, hinged wire grills. Cook about 4 inches from moderately hot coals for 8 minutes. Baste with sauce. Turn and cook for 7 to 10 minutes longer or until fish flakes easily when tested with a fork. Serves 6.

Salmon Casserole

2 salmon steaks
2 teaspoons salt
¼ teaspoon pepper
¼ cup flour
4 tablespoons butter
2 cups sliced onions
1 cup chopped green pepper
3 stalks celery, chopped
2 tablespoons cornstarch
2 cups chicken broth made with bouillon
1 cup canned corn kernels
2 tablespoons soy sauce
1 teaspoon sugar
7 oz. spaghetti noodles, cooked and drained

Cut salmon in 2 inch cubes discarding bones. Dip cubes in mixture of flour, salt, and pepper, coating all sides—in butter saute the salmon, onions, green pepper and celery 10 minutes. Mix cornstarch and broth until smooth. Add to skillet, stirring constantly until it reaches the boiling point, then cook over low heat 5 minutes. Taste for seasoning.

Spread spaghetti in buttered casserole and arrange salmon over it. Pour sauce over all. Cover the casserole.

Bake in 350° oven with cover on for 30 minutes. Remove cover and cook 5 minutes.

Baked Salmon Rolls with Cheese Sauce

3 tablespoons butter
3 tablespoons flour
1½ cups light cream

1 cup grated Cheddar cheese
1 tablespoon sweet sherry
1½ teaspoons salt
6 fillets salmon steak
½ cup grated onion
1 tablespoon lemon juice
½ teaspoon white pepper
¼ cup melted butter

Melt 3 tablespoons butter in a skillet. Mix in flour until smooth. Gradually add the cream, stirring until it reaches the boiling point. Cook over low heat 5 minutes. Add the cheese, sherry and ½ teaspoon salt; cook until cheese melts. Remove from heat.

Roll up salmon; fasten with toothpicks. Arrange in buttered baking dish. Sprinkle with onions, lemon juice, pepper and remaining salt. Pour the ¼ cup melted butter over top.

Bake in 400° oven for 35 minutes. Pour the cheese sauce over the fish and brown under broiler.

French Toasted Salmon Sandwiches

8 oz. cooked salmon
2 tablespoons finely chopped celery
2 green onions, chopped
12 slices of bread
½ cup milk
¼ teaspoon salt
butter or margarine
2 hard cooked eggs, diced
2 tablespoons cocktail sauce or ketchup
2 tablespoons mayonnaise
3 eggs, slightly beaten
¼ cup milk
1½ cups crushed potato chips

Flake salmon and combine with hard cooked eggs, celery, green onion, ketchup and mayonnaise. Spread filling on 6 slices of bread. Top with remaining 6 slices bread. Combine eggs, milk and salt. Dip sandwiches in egg mixture, then in crushed potato chips. Brown sandwiches on both sides in a small amount of butter or margarine on medium hot griddle.
Makes 6 sandwiches.

Beverly Pringle • Portland, Oregon

SMELT

Bacon Wrapped Smelt

Serves 6
2 pounds pan-dressed smelt
or other small fish
2 tablespoons lemon juice
2 teaspoons salt
¼ teaspoon pepper
1 pound sliced bacon
Clean, wash and dry fish. Brush inside of fish with lemon juice and sprinkle with salt and pepper. Wrap each fish with a slice of bacon. Place in well greased, hinged wire grills. Cook about 5 inches from moderately hot coals for 10-15 minutes or until bacon is crisp. Turn and cook for 10 minutes longer or until bacon is crisp and fish flakes easily.

Smelt, Italian Style

Serves 6
2 cups sliced onion
2 cloves garlic, minced
¼ cup melted fat or oil
1 can (1 lb., 12 oz.) Italian tomatoes, undrained
1 can (6 oz.) tomato paste
1½ teaspoons oregano
1½ teaspoons salt
1 teaspoon sugar
¼ teaspoon pepper
¼ cup chopped parsley
2 pounds dressed smelt
1 cup shredded mozzarella cheese
¼ cup shredded Parmesan cheese
Cook onion and garlic in melted fat or oil until onion is tender. Add tomatoes, tomato paste, oregano, 1 teaspoon salt, sugar and pepper; mix well. Cover and cook slowly, about 30 minutes, until slightly thickened and flavors blend; stir often during cooking. Stir in parsley. Spread sauce over bottom of 2-3 quart shallow, rectangular baking dish. Arrange smelt in a single layer on sauce down the center of baking dish. Sprinkle with remaining ½ teaspoon salt and cheeses. Bake in hot oven, 400 degrees F 15-20 minutes or until fish flakes easily when tested with a fork.

Sesame Smelt

Serves 6
2 pounds pan-dressed smelt
(approximately 15 per pound)
1½ teaspoons salt
dash pepper
1 cup pancake mix
½ cup flour
¼ cup yellow cornmeal
1¼ cup milk
1 jar (2 1/8 or 2¼ oz.) sesame seeds

Clean, wash and dry fish. Sprinkle inside and out with salt and pepper. Combine pancake mix, cornmeal, salt and pepper. Add milk and stir only until blended. Stir in sesame seeds. Roll fish in flour and dip in batter. Place in a single layer in a fry basket. Fry in deep fat, 350 degrees F for 3-4 minutes or until golden brown and fish flakes easily when tested with a fork. Drain on absorbent paper. Keep warm.

Smelt Smokies

Serves 4
1½ to 2 pounds cleaned smelt
½ cup flour
¼ cup cornmeal
2 tablespoons smoked salt (2½ table-spoons if more smokey taste is desired)
3 tablespoons dry milk powder
2 teaspoons horseradish (optional)

Clean and wash fish thoroughly. Smelt may be soaked in lemon juice for 15 minutes if desired. Drain fish. Dry mix the remaining listed ingredients and then place in plastic bag. Put fish in bag and shake well to coat thoroughly. Shake off excess mix. Fry in deep fat (peanut oil suggested), at least two inches deep, at 370 degrees until nicely browned on both sides. The same dry mix may be used for shallow pan frying.

Barbecue Sauce:
(Optional use with smelt smokies)
¼ cup ketchup
1 tablespoon taragon vinegar or lemon juice
2 tablespoons horseradish
dash of Tabasco

Mix ingredients thoroughly. Serve on smelt smokies. Sauce is suitable for use with other fried fish.

Conservation Department, Lansing • E. Englehard

Smelt in Tomato Sauce

8 pounds fresh, cleaned smelt
½ cup vinegar
⅔ cup salad oil
2 cups strained tomatoes
2 chili peppers
¼ cup whole allspice
2 bay leaves
2 tablespoons whole cloves
salt to taste

Pack smelt into hot jars. Mix together sauce ingredients but do not cook and pour sauce over smelt to cover. Process pints 50 minutes and quarts 60 minutes at 10 pounds pressure.

Pickled Smelt

Clean smelt and wash; cut into 2'' pieces. Place a 2'' deep layer of fish in crock, then cover with a layer of coarse, non-iodized salt. Add another layer of fish, then salt until you have the amount desired. Place a plate of fish in the crock and place a little weight on plate to hold fish under the liquid that forms in the crock.

Cover crock with cloth and let stand for 2 weeks. After 2 weeks rinse off surplus salt on fish but do not soak. Empty salt from crock and cover fish with cider vinegar. Let stand for 4-5 days.

Drain off vinegar and pack fish in sterilized jars. Cut onion in slices and place a slice in each jar of fish. Add a few pickling spices to each jar and fill jar with fresh vinegar. Add a few drops of oil to keep top of jar of fish moist.

If you prefer, you can add sweet wine to the vinegar when packing in the jars, about half and half.

Sweet Pickled Smelt

Approximately 20 pounds of smelt
Clean and cut in 1 inch pieces. Layer fish and rock salt in a glass or crock container for 48 hours. Then wash and rinse.

Boil together the following:
2 quarts white vinegar
4 tablespoons pickling spices
2 teaspoons alum
2 tablespoons dry mustard
4 tablespoons brown sugar

Let cool—put smelt in jar with layers of onion and add pickling. I like to add a small amount of hot peppers to mine.

Donald Wiese • Vancouver, WA

Batter-Fried Smelt

Flavor is improved by use of milk in their preparation and cooking.

5-6 inch fish are soaked in milk for ½ hour before frying. Dip smelt in batter of 2 eggs, 3 tablespoons rich cream and enough sifted bread crumbs to bind. Season with salt and pepper before frying in deep fat.

Grand Traverse Cream

2 cups steamed flaked sucker
¼ cup green pepper
4 tablespoons flour
2 cups milk
½ cup chopped mushrooms
2 tablespoons chopped onions
4 tablespoons shortening
1 teaspoon salt
dash cayenne

Melt shortening in heavy skillet, add onion and green pepper and cook 2 minutes. Blend in flour and seasonings. Slowly add milk and cook until thickened. Carefully add mushrooms and fish, and heat thoroughly.

Marengo Mustard Magic

2 cups steamed flaked sucker
4 tablespoons flour
2 cups milk
4 tablespoons shortening
1 teaspoon salt
3 teaspoons prepared mustard

Melt shortening in double boiler. Blend in flour and salt. Slowly add milk and cook until thickened; then add mustard and mix thoroughly. Carefully stir in fish, and heat 12-15 minutes. Makes 4-5 servings.

Cooks Corners Original

2 pounds sucker fillets
½ cup butter
¼ cup chopped celery
2 tablespoons shortening or salad oil
1 teaspoon sugar
salt and pepper
1 small onion, chopped
¼ cup chopped green pepper

2 cups canned tomatoes, drained

Preheat oven to 325° F. Place fillets in greased pan; sprinkle with salt, pepper, and butter; bake 15 minutes. Meanwhile, cook onion, celery and green pepper in shortening 2 minutes; then add tomatoes. Season with sugar, salt and pepper, and simmer 10 minutes. Spread; bake 6 minutes.

Grand River Gambol

4 oz. (dry) macaroni
½ to ¾ cup water
1 to 2 medium onions, diced
1 teaspoon salt
1 can undiluted condensed tomato soup
1½ cups steam flaked sucker
few grains pepper
1 cup grated Cheddar, Parmesan or American cheese

Cook macaroni until tender. Preheat oven to 350° F. Combine water and soup. Add remaining ingredients. Place mixture in greased baking dish. Sprinkle with cheese. Bake 30 minutes.

Merriweather Marinade

2 cups steamed flaked sucker
½ cup diced celery
salt
¼ cup chopped green pepper
2 hard-cooked eggs, diced
½ to 1 cup mayonnaise
¼ cup vinegar
1 teaspoon grated onion
1 teaspoon salt
Marinade:
Mix:
1 cup salad oil
¼ cup lemon juice
few grains cayenne

Let fish stand in marinade one hour; then drain well. Combine with green pepper, celery and eggs. Carefully toss this mixture. Season to taste, moisten with mayonnaise, and chill. Makes 4-5 servings.

Dollarville Steak

2 to 2½ pounds skinned sucker fillets
½ teaspoon dry mustard
¼ teaspoon Worcestershire sauce
salt and pepper
2 tablespoons chili sauce
1 teaspoon lemon juice

Place fillets on preheated, greased broiler rack. Mix remaining ingredients.

Spread mixture over fish. Broil until tender. Serves 2.

Timbales New Haven

2 cups steamed flaked carp or sucker
1 cup soft bread crumbs
2 egg yolks
1 tablespoon butter
½ cup milk
2 teaspoons minced onion
2 stiffly-beaten egg whites
4 teaspoons lemon juice

Preheat oven to 350° F. Cook bread crumbs in milk until smooth and thick. Add seasonings, butter and fish. Stir in egg yolks. Fold mixture into egg whites. Fill greased custard cups, set in pan of hot water, and bake 30-35 minutes. Serve with horseradish or sauce of your choice.

Trout Italian

6 pan-dressed rainbow trout or other small dressed fish
½ cup tomato sauce
2 packages (¾ oz. each) garlic-cheese salad dressing mix.
2 tablespoons melted fat or oil
2 tablespoons chopped parsley
2 tablespoons grated Parmesan cheese

Clean, wash and dry thawed fish. Combine remaining ingredients except cheese. Brush fillets inside and out with sauce. Place in a well-greased baking dish, 14 x 9 x 2 inches. Brush with remaining sauce and sprinkle with cheese. Let stand for 30 minutes. Bake in a moderate oven, 350 degrees F for 25-30 minutes or until fish flakes easily when tested with a fork. Turn over control to broil. Place fish about 3 inches from source of heat and broil for 1-2 minutes or until crisp and lightly browned.

Baked Lake Trout with Spinach and Bread Stuffing

Serves 8
3-4 pound dressed lake trout
2½ teaspoons salt
1½ cups thinly sliced celery
¼ cup sliced green onions
½ cup butter or margarine, melted
4 cups soft bread crumbs (½ inch cubes)
4 cups fresh spinach leaves, washed and drained
1 tablespoon lemon juice
¼ teaspoon pepper

Clean, wash and dry fish. Sprinkle inside and out with 1½ teaspoon salt. Cook celery and onion in 6 tablespoons butter or margarine until celery is tender. Stir in bread cubes and spinach leaves. Cook and stir until spinach is tender. Add lemon juice, remaining 1 teaspoon salt, and pepper; toss lightly. Stuff fish loosely. Close opening with small skewers. Place fish in well-greased baking pan. Brush with remaining butter or margarine. Bake in moderate oven, 350 degrees F, 40-60 minutes or until fish flakes easily when tested with a fork.

Rainbow Trout with Mushroom-Herb Stuffing

6 pan-dressed rainbow trout
2 teaspoons salt
4 cups (½ inch) soft bread cubes
⅔ cup butter or margarine
1 cup sliced fresh mushrooms
½ teaspoon marjoram
⅔ cup sliced green onions
¼ cup chopped parsley
2 tablespoons chopped pimento
4 teaspoons lemon juice

Clean, wash and dry fish. Sprinkle 1½ teaspoons salt evenly over inside and outside of fish. Saute bread cubes in ½ cup butter or margarine, until lightly browned, stirring frequently. Add mushrooms and onion. Cook until mushrooms are tender. Stir in remaining salt, parsley, pimento, lemon juice and marjoram; toss lightly. Stuff fish, and arrange in single layer in a well-greased baking pan. Brush with remaining melted butter or margarine. Bake in a moderate oven, 350 degrees F, 25-30 minutes, or until fish flakes easily.

Serve plain or with favorite fish sauce.

Baked Trout in Tomatoes

Grease baking dish—add trout and 6 fresh tomatoes, sliced. If fresh tomatoes are not in season, use 3 cups cooked canned tomatoes. Lightly brown 2 small onions and add to tomatoes. Bake for 40 minutes in 425° oven.

Pan Fried Trout

Serves 4
1 egg
2 tablespoons fresh lemon juice
⅔ cup cornmeal
1 teaspoon salt
¼ teaspoon pepper
4 whole pan-dressed trout
1 lemon, cut in 8 wedges
butter
fresh lemon juice

Slightly beat egg and 2 tablespoons lemon juice in shallow dish. On foil mix together cornmeal, salt and pepper. Dip skin-side of trout in egg mixture, then in cornmeal. Place 2 lemon wedges inside each trout. Close with wooden picks. Melt ¼ cup butter in skillet, add 2 tablespoons lemon juice. Over medium heat fry as many trout as skillet will accommodate, about 8 minutes on each side. Add additional butter and lemon juice as needed.

Sesame Rainbow Trout

Serves 6
6 pan-dressed rainbow trout or other small fish
¼ cup melted fat or oil
¼ cup sesame seeds
2 tablespoons lemon juice
½ teaspoon salt, dash pepper

Clean, wash and dry fish. Combine remaining ingredients. Place fish in a well-greased, hinged wire grill, for cooking outdoors, or under the broiler, when cooking indoors. Baste fish with sauce. Cook about 4 inches from moderately hot coals for 5-8 minutes. Baste with sauce. Turn and cook for 5-8 minutes longer or until fish flakes easily when tested with a fork.

Baked Trout

1 trout approximately 1 pound, cleaned
Leave head on. Place a few slices of onion inside fish with two crushed soda crackers and a liberal dash of ketchup. Lay a slice of bacon on each side of fish, wrap in aluminum foil and bake at moderate heat for 10-15 minutes. Salt to taste.

Mrs. Carl Sisson • Hebo, Oregon

Whitefish Salad

Serves 4-6
½ pound whitefish, cooked
⅓ cup cottage cheese
1 rib celery, diced
1½ tablespoons chopped green pepper
1 tablespoon sweet pickle relish
1 can (29 oz.) peach halves, drained, or 8 fresh peach halves
lettuce

In medium bowl, mix fish, cottage cheese, celery, green pepper and pickle relish. Arrange peach halves in lettuce lined bowl or platter. In small bowl for dressing, mix:
¼ cup lemon juice
1½ teaspoons olive oil
½ teaspoon Dijon mustard
1 tablespoon chopped parsley
¼ teaspoon dill weed
dash garlic powder
dash onion powder
dash paprika
dash salt
dash pepper

Stir this into the fish mixture. Spoon the salad into peach halves. Next time, try filling avacado halves with the fish mixture.

Whitefish Livers

(if you can get 'em)

Once rated an expensive delicacy at the old Blackstone Hotel in Chicago, this wonderful dish has disappeared and few today, even among gourmets, have ever heard of it. On Beaver Island years ago I used to hire young Indian boys to salvage the livers from the cleaning boards as commercial catches of whitefish were cleaned, and treat the entire dining room of the old King Strang Hotel to a marvelous dish. Fry 'em as you would fry chicken livers. You have never eaten anything more delicate and tasty. Salmon livers are worth trying, too. I once tasted them in a Quebec fishing camp, and they came close to matching the whitefish variety.

Ben East • Outdoor Life

Whitefish Amandine

Serves 6
2 pounds whitefish fillets
2 tablespoons lemon juice
2 teaspoons salt
dash pepper
2 tablespoons chopped parsley
½ cup flour
⅓ cup melted fat or oil
½ cup blanched, slivered almonds

Cut thawed fish into serving size portions. Sprinkle fish with lemon juice, salt and pepper. Roll in flour. Fry in hot fat at moderate heat until brown on one side. Turn carefully and brown the other side. Cooking time approximately 10-12 minutes, depending on thickness of fish. Remove fish to hot platter. Fry almonds until lightly browned. Add parsley. Serve over fish.

Lemon Rice Stuffed Whitefish

Serves 6
3-4 pounds dressed whitefish or other fish
1½ teaspoons salt
Lemon rice stuffing
2 tablespoons melted fat or oil

Clean, wash and dry fish. Sprinkle inside and out with salt. Stuff fish loosely. Close opening with small skewers or toothpicks. Place fish on well-greased bake and serve platter, 16 x 10 inches. Brush with fat. Bake in moderate oven 350 degrees for 40-60 minutes or until fish flakes easily when tested with a fork. Baste occasionally with fat. Remove skewers.

Lemon Rice Stuffing:
¾ cup chopped celery
½ cup chopped onion
¼ cup melted fat or oil
1⅓ cups water
2 tablespoons grated lemon rind
1 teaspoon paprika
1 teaspoon salt
dash thyme
1½ cups precooked rice
⅓ cup sour cream
¼ cup diced peeled lemon

Cook celery and onion in fat until tender. Add water, lemon rind, salt, paprika and thyme; bring to a boil. Add rice and stir to moisten. Cover and remove from heat. Let stand 5-10 minutes or until liquid is absorbed. Add sour cream and lemon; mix lightly.

Parade-Dressed Whitefish

Serves 6
2 pounds whitefish fillets or other fish fillets
1 teaspoon salt
dash pepper
cheese stuffing
paprika
2 tablespoons melted fat or oil

Thaw frozen fillets. Sprinkle fillets with salt and pepper. Place half of fillets, skin side down, in a well-greased baking dish, 12 x 8 x 2". Place stuffing on fish and cover with remaining fillets. Brush fish with fat and sprinkle with paprika. Bake in a moderate oven, 350 degrees for 30-35 minutes or until fish flakes easily when tested with a fork.

Cheese Stuffing:
1 cup chopped onion
¼ cup melted fat or oil
2 cups toasted or dry bread cubes
1 cup grated Cheddar cheese
2 tablespoons chopped parsley
2 teaspoons powdered mustard
½ teaspoon salt
dash pepper

Barbecued Whitefish Fillets

Makes 6 servings
2 pounds fish fillets
¼ cup chopped onion
2 tablespoons chopped green pepper
1 clove garlic, finely chopped
2 tablespoons melted fat or oil
2 teaspoons salt
1 can (8 oz.) tomato sauce
2 tablespoons lemon juice
1 tablespoon Worcestershire sauce
1 tablespoon sugar
¼ teaspoon pepper

Cook onion, green pepper and garlic in fat until tender. Add remaining ingredients and simmer for 5 minutes, stirring occasionally. Cool. Cut fish into 6 portions. Place fish in a single layer in a shallow baking dish. Pour sauce over fish and let stand for 30 minutes, turning once. Remove fish, reserving sauce for basting. Place fish in a well-greased, hinged, wire grill. Cook about 4 inches from moderately hot coals for 5-8 minutes. Baste with sauce. Turn. Cook for 5-8 minutes longer or until fish flakes easily when tested with a fork.

Whitefish with Mushroom and Wine Sauce

Serves 6
2 pounds whitefish fillets
3 tablespoons butter or margarine
2 tablespoons lemon juice
1 1/8 teaspoons salt
2 slices bacon, diced
¼ cup sliced green onions
¼ cup water
1 small clove garlic, finely minced
½ cup fresh or canned mushrooms, sliced
1 teaspoon flour
¼ cup ketchup
¼ cup dry white wine

Arrange fillets in single layer in well-buttered baking pan. Drizzle 2 tablespoons melted butter or margarine and lemon juice over fish, and sprinkle with 1 teaspoon salt. Broil 4 inches away from heat source about 10 minutes, or until fish flakes easily when tested with a fork. While fish is broiling, fry bacon until crisp. Remove bacon pieces from pan; drain on absorbent paper. Add 1 tablespoon butter or margarine to bacon pieces from pan. Cook green onion and garlic in drippings until tender. Stir in mushrooms and flour. Add ketchup, wine, water, and 1/8 teaspoon salt. Cook, stirring constantly, until sauce is slightly thickened. Spoon sauce over fish, sprinkle with bacon pieces.

Deviled Whitefish

Serves 6
2 pounds whitefish fillets or other fish fillets
¼ cup chili sauce
2 tablespoons melted fat or oil
2 tablespoons prepared mustard
2 tablespoons grated onion
1 tablespoon lemon juice
1 teaspoon salt
1 teaspoon Worcestershire sauce
dash pepper
chopped parsley

Thaw frozen fillets. Cut into serving-size portions. Combine remaining ingredients except parsley; mix thoroughly. Place fish, skin side up, on a well-greased broiler pan and brush with sauce. Broil about 3 inches from source of heat for 4-5 minutes. Turn carefully and brush other side with sauce. Broil 4-5 minutes longer, basting occasionally, until fish flakes easily when tested with a fork.

DOVE
DUCK
GOOSE
GROUSE
PARTRIDGE
PHEASANT
QUAIL
TURKEY
WOODCOCK

BIRDS

The same rule applies to birds in the field as to other meat—bleed them as quickly after killing them as possible. If you can't bleed your bird immediately, let it cool quickly by letting it lie where there is sufficient air circulating.

FIELD DRESSING

One way to field dress a bird is to pluck a line of feathers from the breastbone to the vent, then make a shallow cut along the line, encircling the vent. Take care not to puncture the intestines. You can then bring out the viscera intact through the split. Rinse the cavity with cold water to remove all the blood.

PLUCKING

It is easiest to dry pluck a bird when the body temperature is high. Pluck feathers in the same direction they are growing to avoid tearing the skin. Pull out as much of the down and feathers with a knife and your thumb as you can. Singe off the remaining down with an open flame.

If you must wait to pluck your bird, you can loosen its feathers by dipping it in scalding water.

Never freeze an unplucked bird. It will be very difficult to pluck when thawed.

Ducks and geese, which are especially difficult to dry pluck, can be dipped in a solution of melted paraffin and water. When the paraffin hardens, strip it off, and all the feathers will come with it. The wax can be used all season by straining it to remove the feathers.

SKINNING

Sometimes it's easier to skin a bird than pluck it, but be careful not to tear the meat. While skinning, keep the thin transparent membrane between skin and meat intact. Remove the oil sacs on either side of the spine just above the tail.

BONING

Place the bird, breast side down, on a cutting board. Using a short, sharp-pointed knife cut a slit through the skin the entire length of the bird along the backbone. Carefully cut the meat away from the bone, following the contours of the backbone.

Sever the joint where the thigh is connected to the skeleton with a knife or poultry shears, being careful not to cut through the meat or skin. Repeat on the other side.

Slip the knife through the joint between the wing bone and the carcass, being careful not to cut all the way through the skin. Repeat on the other side.

After you have freed both the wings and the legs from the carcass, continue to work the meat free, first from one side of the body, then from the other, until the center front of the breastbone is reached. Here, take great care in freeing the skin without piercing it. You should now be able to remove the backbone, breastbone and ribcage in one piece. Place it in the stock pot with the giblets, livers and neck.

Scrape the meat away from the thigh bone. Cut it off at the joint between it and the leg bone. Pull the leg bone away from the meat. Place the bone in the stock pot. Repeat on the other side.

Cut off the second joint of the wing and put it in the stock pot. Pull the wing bone through from the inside, bringing the skin with it. Scrape away the meat. Put the bone in the stock pot. Repeat on the other side.

Check to be sure no tiny bits of bone remain.

OLD OR YOUNG?

If your bird can be lifted by its lower beak without having it break, it is mature and somewhat tougher than a young bird. The breastbone of a bird hardens as it matures; if the breastbone indents when you poke it, it is a young bird. Also, the claws on an older bird are blunter than those on a young bird. An old bird should be cooked longer, braised, or tenderized to improve the texture. One trick is to sprinkle commercial tenderizer in the cavity of an old bird. Be sure to label your bird as to its age before you put it in the freezer.

AGING

Game birds should be hung for four to six days at a temperature of 35° to 40°. This will lessen the gamey taste, as well as tenderize the meat.

Trim the outside fat on water fowl to reduce the fishy taste.

Most of the meat on ducks is on the breast and thighs; the back, wings and drumsticks are hardly worth serving.

FREEZING

Turn to the "Freezer Tips" and "Freezer Storage" sections of the "Big Game" chapter for information.

DOVE

Dove meat is dark and flavorful. Cook it slowly and with plenty of moisture to counter its tendency to be tough. Plan on preparing one dove per person.

Roast Dove

Place cleaned whole dove, or dove breast in baking dish just large enough to accommodate one layer of birds, breast side up. Sprinkle with salt and pepper to taste, and add about ½ teaspoon poultry seasoning for each 12 birds. Chop 1 large onion, 2 stalks celery and 1 apple (unpared). Distribute over birds. Add ¼ cup water and dot with 1 stick margarine. Bake 30 minutes in 325 degree oven, remove and turn breast side down. Return to oven for approximately 30 minutes more for young dove and 45 minutes for older birds or until tender.

If doves were skinned instead of plucked, pan should be covered with foil last 30 minutes to keep it from drying out.

Catawba County Wildlife Club • Joan Wilfong

Sauteed Dove

Split birds down the back. Dust lightly with flour and saute in butter. Brown quickly on skin side, turn and cook on bone side and turn again. Reduce heat and continue cooking until birds are tender.

Depending on size of birds, it will take from 15-20 minutes. Season birds with salt and pepper to taste. Remove birds from skillet and add ½ cup dry white wine to drippings. Bring to a boil and serve as clear gravy.

DUCK

Dress a duck very soon after shooting. Wipe the body cavity and internal organs with a cloth wrung out in hot water, instead of holding the bird under running water. This prevents flavor from being lost. Soak your duck for 45 to 60 minutes in a solution of ½ cup salt and ½ cup vinegar added to enough water to cover the bird. This will remove strong flavors and blood clots.

Ducks tend to dry out with roasting, so keep the skin on (removing the feathers, of course) to preserve the juices.

Duck heart, liver and gizzard are delicious in gravy or stuffing.

Duck meat is best when cooked on the rare side.

Generally, one duck will serve two people.

In slicing cooked duck, use a sharp knife and slice the breast meat straight sideways instead of down. This gives wider slices and less breaking up.

Roast Wild Duck with Sausage Stuffing

Fills 2 ducks
¼ cup finely chopped onion
¼ cup butter
¼ cup finely chopped celery
3 cups cubed, day old bread
½ teaspoon poultry seasoning
1/8 teaspoon black pepper
¼ teaspoon salt
½ cup milk
1 egg, beaten
¼ pound pure pork sausage

Add onions and celery to butter which has been melted in saucepan. Cook until transparent and yellow. To this add bread and seasoning. Toss lightly to coat with butter. Remove from heat. Add pork sausage. Combine milk and egg and drizzle over bread mixture. Stir lightly to blend. Pack into salted cavity of the bird. Close filled cavity with skewers or tooth-picks. Place in roasting pan and brush breast with melted butter or margarine. Place pan in preheated 325 degree oven. Repeat butter brushing every 10-15 minutes for ¾ of an hour. Cover roasting pan for final hour of cooking. Allow ducks to bake for a total of 1½ to 2½ hours or until tender.

Saucy Orange Duckling

2 2 pound ducks, cut in pieces
½ cup orange juice
2 teaspoons salt
1 teaspoon beef seasoning base
¼ teaspoon pepper
½ cup orange marmalade
2 tablespoons light sherry
¼ cup flour
hot cooked brown rice (optional)

In four-quart pressure cooker, brown duckling a few pieces at a time until lightly browned. Spoon off fat as it accumulates. Remove duckling and pour off all fat. Place rack in bottom of pressure cooker. Add duckling, orange juice, salt, beef, seasoning base and pepper. Cover and lock. Place regulator on air vent at 15 pounds pressure. Cook over high heat until regulator starts to rock. Reduce heat. Cook 15 minutes. Remove from heat and reduce pressure quickly under running cold water. Remove cover. Reserve duck and pan juices.

Meanwhile, in small saucepan, melt marmalade over low heat. Stir in sherry. Set aside. Place cooked duckling on broiler pan. Place under broiler until well-browned. Brush marmalade sauce over ducks. Broil until bubbling and glazed.

Wild Duck Detroit Club-Style

Serves 6
3 wild ducks, dressed, cleaned
6 ribs celery, washed
salt, pepper
about 1½ quarts well-seasoned bread stuffing
1 cup water
½ cup dry red wine
¼ cup orange marmalade
¼ cup currant jelly
1 thin-skinned juice orange diced, rind and all
½ lemon, diced rind and all
1 tablespoon bottle browning and seasoning salt
dash tarragon
well-seasoned chicken broth (about 2 quarts)

Preheat oven to 450 degrees. Run cold water quickly through inside of duck to clean it. Sprinkle with salt and pepper and place 2 ribs of celery in each cavity. Roast uncovered, breast-side-up about 30 minutes, until golden brown. Remove from oven. Reduce oven temperature to 400 degrees. Pull out celery. Let blood and juices drain out. Discard any drippings. Let ducks cool slightly. Stuff. Place breast-side down in roasting pan. Place water, wine, marmalade, jelly, orange, lemon, browning and seasoning salt and tarragon in pan. Add enough chicken broth to just about cover ducks. Cover pan loosely with aluminum foil. Bake in a 400 degree oven until tender (leg will move easily), about 3 hours. Remove ducks from pan; keep warm.

Skim fat off gravy. Reduce gravy by boiling. Thicken with flour dissolved in water, if desired. Strain. Serve over ducks.

Orange-Roasted Duck

Serves 2 generously
2 mallards
salt, pepper
½ stick butter
juice and rind of 1 orange

Clean ducks thoroughly, dry. Rub lightly with salt and pepper, inside and out. Brown in melted butter in a frying pan. Transfer to a roasting pan. Pour orange juice in the cavities of the birds, and arrange the peeling around the outside.

Cover and bake at 300 degrees until tender.

Remove ducks and make gravy from the pan drippings.

Duck and Dressing

2 mallards or 4 wood ducks
3 cups seasoned bread stuffing
¼ cup diced celery
1 large apple, pared and cubed
½ cup raisins or prunes

Moisten stuffing with hot water; add apple, celery and raisins or prunes. Toss lightly until mixed. Salt cavity of ducks, and fill with stuffing. Place, breast side up, in roasting pan. Cover; bake at 325 degrees about 2 hours for small ducks or 3 hours for large ducks.

Catawba County Wildlife Club • Joan Wilfong

Quick Roasted Wild Duck

Place ½ orange inside cavity of each duck. Place the ducks on a rack in a shallow pan and roast in 450 to 475 degree oven. Baste ducks well with melted butter and red or white wine or with melted butter and orange juice. Roast for 20-30 minutes. Season with salt and pepper.

Baked Wild Duck in Brown-in-Bag

1 duck
melted butter or margarine
salt
chopped apple and celery
1 tablespoon flour
1 cup orange juice
preheat oven to 350 degrees

Shake 1 tablespoon flour in small size (10″ x 16″) brown-in-bag and place in 2″ deep roasting pan. Pour orange juice into bag and stir until flour is well mixed. Brush duck with butter. Salt cavity and outside. Fill cavity with chopped apple and celery. Place duck in bag. Close bag with twist tie and make 6 ½″ slits in top. Cook 1½ hours.

Duck Adam

Serves 4

Two ducks will serve four people if they are mallards or canvasbacks, if it is boned, sprinkled with apple brandy, dipped in crushed peppercorns, and sauteed. Serve with a creamy brandy sauce, pureed turnips and a green salad with tart dressing. Make duck stock by placing duck bones, heart, giblets and neck in stock pot with onion, carrot, parsley and soup spices. Cover with water and simmer at least an hour.

1 boned duck
¼ teaspoon thyme
salt to taste
½ cup apple brandy
⅓ cup peppercorns, crushed
3 tablespoons butter
1 tablespoon oil
1 cup duck stock
¼ cup heavy cream

Cut the boneless ducks into four serving pieces. Trim away excess fat reserving one small piece. Sprinkle each half of duck with thyme and salt. Splash on about three tablespoons apple brandy. Coat both sides of each piece with crushed peppercorns. (A blender crushes peppercorns easily). Melt butter, oil and reserved duck fat in a large skillet. Add duck skin-side down. Saute about 15 minutes. Turn over and saute an additional 10 minutes, until well browned and cooked through. (Don't overcook as it becomes tough.) Warm remaining apple brandy, pour over duck and flame. When flames subside, remove duck to a serving platter and keep warm. Pour off most of the fat in the skillet. Add duck stock. Bring to a boil; simmer until sauce is reduced about one third. Add heavy cream, stirring constantly until slightly thickened. Strain. Serve sauce separately with duck.

Duck Casserole

2 small wild ducks
flour
shortening
8 small boiling onions
1 cup mushrooms
4 cups water
2 teaspoons salt
¼ teaspoon pepper
2 teaspoons seasoned salt
2 cups carrots, sliced round
1 package frozen peas
1/8 teaspoon savory

Cut ducks into serving pieces, flour lightly and brown very slowly in shortening. Remove pieces of duck to greased casserole. Brown onions and mushrooms very lightly in fat. Arrange over duck. Add 4 tablespoons flour to fat and blend. Add water and cook and stir until boiling. Add salt, pepper and seasoned salt. Pour over duck. Cover casserole and bake in moderate oven at 350° for 1 hour. Add carrots, peas and savory, cover and continue baking 1 hour.

Serve with rice.

Eleanor Makinster • Rainier, Oregon

Buckley Duck

1 duck (1½ pounds)
2 cups quartered apples
1 slice of onion
2 teaspoons salt
¼ teaspoon pepper
Cooking time about 45 minutes

Clean duck and wash thoroughly. Fill the duck with peeled quartered apples. Sew up and tie in shape. Rub with a slice of onion, then salt and pepper. Roast uncovered in a moderately slow oven (325°) allowing 20 to 30 minutes per pound. If desired, duck can be basted every 10 minutes with 1 cup of orange juice. Basting is not required, however, at this low temperature.

Duck with Apples and Raisins

2 mallard ducks
6 medium-sized tangy apples
1 cup seeded raisins
4 tablespoons ham or bacon drippings
1 teaspoon mixed pickling spices
4 strips bacon

Rub ducks inside and out with salt, place breast up on a rack in a roaster. Quarter the apples, stuff several pieces and a small handful of raisins into each duck, pin a strip of bacon across each breast.

Put the rest of the apples and raisins and the pickling spices around the ducks, add the ham or bacon fat. Add a mixture of one part Sauterne or sherry wine and three parts water to come about half-way up the ducks (I put in 1 cup of wine and 3 cups of water, and repeat until I have enough). Cover and bake in moderate (300°) oven 1½ hours. Remove lid and bake in hot oven (450°) until brown— about ½ hour. When properly cooked, the meat should readily come away from the breast and rib bones—the breast, wing and leg on each side coming away in one piece. Serves four.

Mike Brown • Muskegon, MI

Barbecued Breast of Duck

Remove breast meat in one whole piece for each side. Broil near flame or coals until brown, about 10 minutes. While broiling, baste frequently with barbecue sauce containing lemon juice, Worcestershire sauce, ketchup and butter. When meat begins to brown, sprinkle with salt and paprika; continue broiling until done.

Left-over Duck

½ package pastry mix
¼ cup fat
1 (8 oz.) can small whole onions
1 (10½ oz.) can chicken consomme
1/8 teaspoon pepper
1 teaspoon Kitchen Bouquet
1 (8¾ oz.) can diced carrots
2 cups diced cooked duck
½ cup celery, diced
¼ cup flour
1 (3 oz.) can chopped broiled mushrooms
1 teaspoon salt
¼ teaspoon marjoram
1 (8½ oz.) can potatoes, diced
1 (8½ oz.) can peas

Prepare pastry mix according to directions on package. Roll out 1/8 inch thick and cut 3 inch circles with biscuit cutter. Place on baking sheet and prick well with tines of fork. Bake 375° until lightly browned, about 10 minutes. Melt fat over moderate heat; add celery and cook 5 minutes. Stir in flour, remove from heat. Drain onions and mushrooms, reserving broth; add consomme to make 2 cups. Add combined broth to fat mixture and cook, stirring constantly, until gravy thickens and comes to a boil. Add seasonings, onions, mushrooms, drained potatoes, carrots, peas and cooked duck. Cover and heat thoroughly, about 10 minutes. When ready to serve, pour duck mixture into hot casserole. Top with circles of pastry and serve at once. Yield: 6 servings.

Chinese Duck

two large ducks
1 cup of apricot preserves
¼ cup of melted butter
apple
soy sauce
½ cup of beer
2 cloves of minced garlic
¼ cup of dry mustard
salt and pepper
lemon juice

Mix the garlic cloves into a paste and liberally add salt and pepper and rub into the ducks. Next, brush the ducks with the melted butter. Put the ducks in a shallow roasting pan, breast up with half an apple in each cavity. Roast in a 400° oven for 15 minutes. Next, mix the mustard, beer, apricots and a dash of soy sauce and lemon juice to taste. Pour this sauce over the ducks and reduce heat to 350° and roast for 30 more minutes. These portions should serve 4.

Chuck Nelson

GOOSE

Dress a goose very soon after shooting.

Do not rinse the cavity with running water because you will lose some flavor. Wipe the cavity with a cloth wrung out in hot water.

A goose tends to dry out when roasting, so keep the skin on to preserve the juices.

Goose heart, liver and gizzard are delicious in gravy or stuffing.

Goose meat is best when rare.

Generally, one goose will serve two people.

Irish Roast Goose

Clean and dry the goose, rub inside and out with salt and pepper mixed at the ratio of 1 teaspoon salt to ¼ teaspoon pepper.
Stuffing:
10 medium potatoes, boiled and diced

1 cup chopped onions
¼ teaspoon pepper
½ pound ground salt pork
1 teaspoon poultry seasoning
1 tablespoon fat
½ cup chopped celery
4 slices bread, crumbed
2 eggs, beaten
1 teaspoon salt

Reserve potato water for basting. Put fat in skillet and partially cook onions and celery, but do not brown. Combine all the ingredients into a stuffing mixture, stuff goose and roast in a moderate oven 3-4 hours, basting from time to time with potato water.

Roast Goose and Stewed Apples

1 goose
salt
4 cups water
6 peppercorns
¼ pound butter
½ onion sliced
2 tablespoons flour
Stewed apples

Remove wings, neck and feet. Cover with cold water and soak for 15 minutes. Drain and pat dry. Rub with salt inside and out.

Put the bird in a roaster, add water, onion and peppercorns. Roast in moderate oven (325°). After the water has boiled down, baste the bird with the butter that has been browned. Allow about 25 minutes per pound. If the goose appears to be an old one, allow an extra 20 minutes to insure complete cooking.

Place the goose on a warmed platter. Put roaster on burner on top of stove, stir in flour, add 2 cups of water and boil for three minutes until smooth and slightly thickened.

Serve the goose and gravy together with the stewed apples.

Stewed Apples

2 pounds apples, peeled and quartered
2 tablespoons butter
½ cup sugar
1 tablespoon lemon juice
½ cup water
¼ cup white wine
1 small piece lemon peel

Stew together until apples are tender and almost transparent, serve hot.

German Goose

1 package goose gizzards, heart and liver
1 large leek
2 bay leaves
2 cups croutons
white wine or dry sherry
2 eggs
nutmeg, thyme
1 pound ground beef
10 cloves, ground
2 apples
10 chestnuts
½ cup raisins
salt, pepper
water and bouillon (or broth)

Finely chop gizzards, heart and liver and saute with one-inch slices of leek. Add ¼ cup of wine. Peel apples, cut into eighths. Add the rest of the ingredients, mix them together and stuff bird. Roast goose at 550° until slightly browned. Then turn down to 350° and baste periodically. An 8-10 pound goose takes two hours while a 10-14 pound goose takes 2½ hours. Remove goose, drain all grease. Pour ¼ cup wine or sherry into drippings and let it completely boil out. Add one tablespoon flour, stir over heat until lightly browned. Add 3 cups cold water or any type of broth. Stirring, bring to a boil. Strain.

Paul Gutterman • East Lansing, MI

GROUSE OR PARTRIDGE

One grouse, or partridge, serves one person, or two if it is large. Patridge has been called "a true gourmet's delight."

Grouse Supreme

1 grouse, quartered, or 4 quail, halved
1½ teaspoons salt
1/8 teaspoon pepper
flour
oil
1 small onion, sliced and ringed
½ cup bias cut celery
½ cup sliced water chestnuts
¼ cup dry white wine
¼ cup water

Dredge meat in flour to which salt and pepper have been added. Cover bottom of skillet with 1/8" oil. Preheat to about 375 degrees. Place meat in hot oil until golden brown. Remove to platter. Place onion and celery in fat and stir fry about three minutes. Reduce heat to 225 degrees. Arrange browned meat over onions and celery. Add water chestnuts, wine and water. Cover and steam until fork tender, about 30 minutes.

Catawba County Wildlife Club • Joan Wilfong

Grouse Au Vin

(Good with pheasant or rabbit)
1 quart port wine
6 whole cloves
6 medium slices onion
1 large bay leaf
1 teaspoon sage
2 cups flour
¼ pound margarine or butter
1½ teaspoons salt
1 teaspoon black pepper
2 birds or 2 rabbits.

After birds have been thoroughly cleaned and singed, cut into pieces as you would a chicken. Combine port wine, cloves, onions, bay leaf and sage. Soak pieces in this wine mixture for 2-3 days, storing in refrigerator.

Drain the birds, reserving the liquid. Wipe dry and dip in flour to which has been added salt and pepper. Brown on both sides in margarine or butter. Turn the birds and the liquid into a casserole. Cover for baking in slow oven, 300 degrees, for 1½ hours, or until tender.

Partridge Breasts in Cheese Sauce

Serves 4
4 partridge breasts
2 cans Cheddar cheese soup
1 small can pimento, sliced
2 slices bacon, crumbled
1 cup milk
flour
salt and pepper

Roll partridge breasts in flour, seasoned with salt and pepper. Brown in bacon fat. Put in casserole dish. Combine soup and milk. Pour over meat. Lay strips of pimento over birds and sprinkle bacon over it all. Bake, covered at 325 degrees for 1¼ hours. Uncover and return to oven to brown cheese.

Partridge Casserole

Serves 4
2 partridge breasts and legs
2 onions, sliced
1 carrot, sliced
1 stalk celery, sliced
1 cup cream of mushroom soup
1 can evaporated milk
1 can mushroom pieces, drained
1 bay leaf
1 cup (dry) wild rice, or brown rice

Simmer partridge with onion, carrot, celery and bay leaf for 20 minutes until tender. Cool. Save stock, skim when cool, and save for cooking rice.

Bone the meat. Mix mushrooms, soup, evaporated milk, 1 teaspoon salt and ¼ teaspoon pepper and fold pieces of meat in. Place in buttered casserole dish. Bake at 350 degrees for 1½ hours. Serve over rice.

Partridge in Tomato Sauce

Serves 2
2 partridges, in serving pieces
1 small can tomato paste
1 small can mushrooms, with juice
¼ cup flour
1 medium onion, diced
½ teaspoon oregano
¼ teaspoon thyme
1 teaspoon parsley flakes
salt and pepper

Dredge partridges in flour seasoned with salt and pepper. Place meat in hot fat and brown well. Add onions and cook until yellow.

Add tomato paste, mushrooms, seasonings, salt and pepper to taste. Simmer slowly for 30 minutes, or until tender. Add water if it begins to dry out.

Camp Birds

2-3 partridges (or pheasants)

salad oil (bacon grease, if using pheasants)
1 small onion chopped fine
1 pound mushrooms, cleaned & sliced lengthwise
¼ cup of brandy and a little more
nutmeg
sweet fern
salt and pepper
½ to 1 cup Jim Beam or chicken broth
1 tablespoon cornstarch or 2 tablespoons flour

Brown partridges in salad oil, or pheasants in bacon grease in skillet. Remove birds and keep warm. To brownings in skillet, add onion and mushrooms. Saute until onions are limp and the mushrooms start to juice. Return birds to pan and flame as follows:

Add ¼ cup of brandy. DO NOT BOIL. Heat one large cooking spoon filled with additional brandy; when almost boiling, light spoonful with a splinter from the fire and pour flaming brandy into skillet. Shake pan continuously until flame burns out. Season with nutmeg (optional), sweet fern, salt (be careful if bacon grease was used) and fresh pepper. Add Jim Beam bourbon or chicken broth. Cover skillet, cook gently for ½ hour or until juices run clear when birds are pierced with a fork.

If desired, thicken sauce with one tablespoon cornstarch or 2 tablespoons pancake flour. Blend smooth with ¼ cup cold water and simmer gently in pan juices. (Remove bird before thickening sauce). Serve with French bread, rice, green salad and fruit conserve.

PHEASANT

Pluck the pheasant if the bird is to be roasted, or it will dry out in the oven.

Pheasant can be cooked just like chicken. It is all white meat. It can also be prepared like quail or turkey.

Generally, one pheasant will serve three or four people.

Baked Pheasant & Rice

Serves 6-8
1 10 oz. can condensed cream of mushroom soup
⅔ cup milk
¾ cup long grain rice, uncooked
1 4 oz. can mushrooms, undrained
one 1½ oz. envelope dehydrated onion soup mix.
2 pheasants, in serving pieces.

Blend mushroom soup and milk. Combine this with rice, mushrooms and juice and onion soup. Mix and pour into 13 x 9 x 2'' baking dish. Arrange pheasant on top. Brush with melted butter, sprinkle with paprika and bake uncovered in oven preheated to 325 degrees for 1½ hours.

Libby Lincoln • Okemos, MI

Baked Pheasant in Foil

1 pheasant
melted butter or margarine
Spice Parisienne (optional) use sparingly
½ orange
½ cup dry white wine
preheat oven 425 degrees

Brush entire surface of bird with melted butter. Sprinkle cavity and surface with salt. Sprinkle very small amount of Spice Parisienne on surface of pheasant. Stuff ½ orange into cavity. Place bird on heavy duty aluminum foil. Bring edges together and seal tightly. Place in shallow roasting pan and bake at 425 degrees for 1¼ hours. Open foil and allow pheasant to brown for another ¼ hour. Remove pheasant and foil from pan and add ½ cup dry white wine to drippings and heat to boiling. Cut pheasant into quarters and serve with the clear wine gravy.

Pheasant and Wine

Roll cut up pheasant in flour, salt and pepper. Brown in hot oil. Bake in oven with 1 cup of wine, and one sliced onion, until done. If it begins to dry out, add water.

Libby Lincoln • Okemos, MI

Baked Pheasant in Brown-in-Bag

1 pheasant
melted butter or margarine
1 tablespoon flour
salt
Spice Parisienne (optional) use sparingly
½ orange
½ cup dry white wine

Preheat oven to 350 degrees. Shake 1 tablespoon flour in small size (10 x 16'') Brown-in-Bag and place in 2'' deep roasting pan. Pour wine into bag and stir until flour is well-mixed. Brush pheasant with melted butter and sprinkle with seasonings. Stuff ½ orange into cavity. Place pheasant in bag. Close bag with twist tie and make six half-inch slits in top. Cook 1½ hours. Cut pheasant in quarters and use juices in bag as gravy.

Herbed Rice with Pheasant

Parboil cut-up pheasant 45-60 minutes. Remove immediately from water and pat dry. Slowly over low heat brown the pheasant pieces in butter. Turn often. While browning pheasant, prepare long grain or brown rice.

In a saucepan, melt ½ cup of butter. To the butter add your favorite seasonings. (Suggest parsley, sage, oregano, seasoned salt, seasoned pepper, celery seed and 1 bay leaf). Cook together 5-7 minutes. Remove bay leaf. Add butter mixture to prepared rice. Cook over low heat 5 minutes, stirring often. Place in serving dish. Top with browned pheasant. Cheese sauce may be used to top entire dish.

Jeannine Staneway

Fried Pheasant

(or rabbit or squirrel)
¼ pound butter
½ medium sized onion
1 quart milk or cream
2 cups flour
1½ teaspoon salt
1 teaspoon black pepper
2 tablespoons flour and ¼ cup milk for gravy

After birds have been thoroughly cleaned and singed, cut into pieces like a chicken. Dust pieces in flour to which has been added salt and pepper. Brown on both sides in butter. Add milk or cream and simmer 1 to 1½ hours or until tender. For a cooking variation, add one small can of condensed cream of mushroom soup to the quart of milk or cream.

Remove pieces from frying pan to prepare gravy. Thicken liquid with batter of 2 tablespoons of flour and ¼ cup of milk. Allow to simmer to desired thicknesses.

Pheasant Exotic

After cleaning the bird, rub it generously with butter and sprinkle on salt and pepper.

Put the pheasant in an uncovered roasting pan, and sear at about 400° to 450° for 10 minutes.

Reduce the heat to about 350°, add one glass of apple cider and roast for about 1 hour, perhaps a little longer depending on the size of the bird.

While the pheasant is roasting, peel several bananas, cut slits in them, and fill the slits with honey or syrup. When the bird is within 15 minutes of being done, add the bananas to the pan. Complete roasting.

Ray K. Williams • MBH member

Pheasant Cacciatore

2 pheasants
½ cup olive oil
1 large carrot, diced
¼ pound butter
1 large can Italian style tomatoes
1 green pepper, seeded and diced
⅔ cup dry sherry or white wine
2 large cloves of garlic, diced
1 box (7 oz.) fresh mushrooms, diced
1 can tomato paste
2 large ribs of celery, diced
1 medium onion, chopped
½ teaspoon oregano (optional)
salt and pepper to taste

Cut pheasant into serving pieces, place in deep baking dish or roaster. Sprinkle over it the garlic, celery, carrot, mushrooms, onion, green pepper. Dot with butter, sprinkle with salt, pepper and oregano. Mix tomatoes with tomato paste and wine and spread all over the pheasant. Pour olive oil evenly over all. Bake in 450° oven 1½ to 2 hours or more until pheasant is tender and the tomato gravy is reduced to just short of being dry. Turn the pieces several times during baking. If the juices don't seem to be cooking up fast enough, or the pheasant browning enough, turn oven heat up to 500° near the end of the baking period.

Pheasant Casserole

2 pheasants
2 small carrots
2 onions, quartered
2 cups cooked rice
½ cup diced ham
2 stalks celery
1 apple, quartered
salt and pepper
2 tablespoons olive oil or vegetable oil

Dress and wash birds well. Season. Stuff with celery, carrots, apples, onions, olive oil and diced ham all mixed thoroughly. Place the birds in a buttered casserole and bake covered until tender and brown.

Pheasant and Sauerkraut

2 pheasants
dash of pepper
2 slices of bacon
½ cup white wine
1 tablespoon flour
1½ teaspoons salt
2 tablespoons butter
1½ pounds sauerkraut
1 cup diced pineapple

Rinse birds, season lightly inside and out with salt and pepper. Place bacon slice on each breast, saute birds in butter for 15 minutes or until brown. Place in casserole. Drain sauerkraut, mix with wine and pineapple and surround the birds. Cover and cook slowly for one hour. When birds are done remove from sauerkraut, remove bacon and place the pheasants on a warm serving dish. Stir flour into kraut and cook a few minutes. Serve the kraut with the birds. Makes three or four servings.

Pheasant or Quail

Draw and clean bird. Cut up pheasant, use quail whole.

1 bird
¼ cup flour
1 teaspoon salt
½ teaspoon pepper
fat
juice 1 lemon

3 tablespoons Worcestershire sauce per 2 pound bird

Combine salt, pepper and flour in paper bag, add bird and shake until coated. Brown bird quickly in 1-inch hot fat. Drain off fat, add Worcestershire sauce and lemon juice. Cover with tight lid and place on very low heat to steam. Turn meat occasionally for about 1 hour or until tender.

Pheasantburger

3 cups pheasant or duck
½ cup ketchup
2 tablespoons olive oil
1 diced onion
1 tablespoon prepared mustard
1 teaspoon onion juice

Using coarse blade, force meat and onion through chopper. Add and mix mustard, pepper, salt and make into patties. Broil, basting with mixture of olive oil, ketchup and onion. Serve on buttered toast or toasted buns.

Pheasant Fricassee, In Cream

Cut pheasant into serving-size pieces. Wipe clean. Fry in lard to a golden brown and add a little water occasionally, dusting the gravy lightly with flour from a shaker. Salt and pepper to taste. Add butter occasionally. When the pheasant is tender and the gravy is rich and thick, transfer to an oven casserole and half cover with rich cream. Cook in a steady oven, but not too hot, until the cream has blended with the gravy and has evaporated somewhat.

Roast Pheasant

Place unplucked, uncleaned bird in brown paper bag 7-10 days. Pluck and clean to make "pan ready."

Salt and pepper cavity. Place heel of French bread in cavity. Roast at 375° for 35 minutes. Add 1 can of pitted olives and juice. Cook 5 minutes longer. Unbelievable? We tried it and the results are outstanding.

Mrs. M. E. Schutz • Redwood City, CA

QUAIL

Quail can be either plucked or skinned. The skin will act to conserve the bird's moisture and flavor.

One quail will generally serve one person.

Starlings can be substituted for quail in any recipe.

Sauteed Quail

Split birds down the back. Dust lightly with flour and saute in butter. Brown quickly on skin side, turn and cook on bone side and turn again. Reduce heat and continue cooking until birds are tender. Depending on size of birds, it will take from 15-20 minutes. Season birds with salt and pepper to taste. Remove birds from skillet and add ½ cup dry white wine to drippings. Bring to a boil and serve as clear gravy.

Hunter's Quail

Serves 4
4 quail
salt and pepper
4 cups shredded cabbage
4 slices bacon cooked crisp, crumbled
16 large cabbage leaves
2 tablespoons butter
1 cup chicken broth
4 small apples, sliced
¼ teaspoon crushed thyme
¼ teaspoon crushed taragon
¼ teaspoon caraway seeds
1 teaspoon salt
¼ teaspoon pepper

Sprinkle quail with salt and pepper. Combine shredded cabbage and bacon and stuff ¼ of mixture in cavity of each bird. Wrap each bird with 4 cabbage leaves and tie with string. Put in Dutch oven on the stove.

In saucepan, put rest of ingredients, simmer for 5 minutes. Pour over birds. Bring liquid to a boil, lower heat, cover and simmer 25-30 minutes until tender. Remove string and cabbage leaves, and serve with the sauce.

Grilled Quail

Split quail in half lengthwise. Baste with lemon butter, to which parsley flakes have been added. Place over charcoal or wood coals and roast about an hour, or until meat pulls away from the bone easily.

Baste frequently with lemon butter.

Quail Veronique

Roast quail and place in serving dish. Add to the roasting pan, minced very fine: 1 carrot, 1 small onion, a stalk of celery, a pinch of thyme, ½ bay leaf. Let simmer. When the vegetables are light brown add 1 glass of dry white wine, 2 cups chicken broth. When boiling thicken sauce with butter (a mixture of two parts butter for one part of flour, blended together and added to liquid). Let cook for 10 minutes on a slow fire. Strain, season to taste and put back on fire. Add 1 cup of fresh peeled and seeded grapes. Pour over quail. Sprinkle with fresh finely chopped parsley. Serve with steamed new potatoes or wild rice.

Quail with Brown Rice

salt, pepper
½ cup flour
3 teaspoons cornmeal
1½ cups brown rice

Combine flour, cornmeal, salt and pepper and roll birds in this mixture. Fry birds to delicious brown and add more salt and pepper. Pour from 6 to 8 ounces of water on quail and cook until tender, keeping a lid on the skillet. Add 6 cups of water to the brown rice and cook until done and then drain the rice. Make a rich gravy from the fat which birds were cooked in, (a quantity of 2½ cups). Add gravy to the rice and serve with the bird.

Quail and Mushrooms

6 quail
1 heaping tablespoon butter
1 teaspoon chopped parsley
1 teaspoon chopped onion
1 tablespoon flour
1 can mushrooms and liquid
1 cup sherry
½ teaspoon pepper
½ teaspoon salt
Tabasco to taste

Brown quail in separate skillet, before adding other ingredients. Place breast down in sauce, simmer ½ hour or until tender. To make the sauce, saute parsley and onion until brown. Add flour and brown it. Then add mushrooms and liquid, sherry, salt and pepper. Cook thoroughly.

Quail Pie

3 quail
½ pound veal steak
1 teaspoon salt
1/8 teaspoon black pepper
6 slices bacon, halved
3 tablespoons flour
2 cups stock or water
2 whole cloves
1 cup sliced mushrooms (optional)
1 tablespoon chopped parsley
½ cup sherry
pastry or biscuit dough

Clean and split birds down the back; cut veal in 6 strips; sprinkle all with salt and pepper and saute in drippings in heavy frying pan until brown. Put birds in casserole, cover with veal and bacon pieces over top. Stir flour into drippings in pan. Add stock and stir and cook until thickened; add cloves and pour the mixture over meat in the casserole. Bake covered in moderate (350°) oven for 1 hour or until tender. Then, place mushrooms on top, sprinkle with parsley, and pour the sherry over all. Put on top of rolled pastry dough or small biscuits.

TURKEY

A wild turkey should be treated the same as a domestic bird.

Roast Wild Turkey

10-12 pound wild turkey, dressed
salt and pepper
garlic powder to taste
3 ribs celery, with leaves
onion, quartered
2 bay leaves
2 pounds pork spare ribs or skin from pork shoulder

Wash and thoroughly dry turkey. Rub cavity and outside with salt, pepper and garlic powder. Place onion, celery and bay leaves in cavity. Place bird on rack in roaster, breast side up. Cover with spare ribs or pork skin. When turkey is done, pork skin will be crisp, and cracklings can be used in corn bread. If spare ribs are used, you will have a delicious second dish.

Roast turkey at 325 degrees for 3-4 hours. Remove pork skin or ribs during last half hour of cooking to allow turkey to brown.

Roast Wild Turkey

A wild turkey would be treated the same as a domestic bird. Keep the stuffing simple and not too highly seasoned. After stuffing the turkey, rub well with butter, salt and pepper. Place it on a rack in a roasting pan. Roast at 325 degrees. Allow 22-25 minutes per pound. Baste the turkey often with equal amounts of butter and white wine.

Turkey Wings Fricassee

Serves 4
4 young turkey wings
flour
2 teaspoons salt
¾ teaspoon paprika
¼ teaspoon pepper
¼ cup butter or shortening
2 medium onions, chopped
1 clove garlic, crushed
4 cups chicken broth
2 carrots, sliced
2 ribs celery, sliced
1 bay leaf
¼ teaspoon rosemary
½ cup cold water
cooked noodles, optional

In shallow dish combine about ¼ cup of the flour, salt, pepper and paprika. Roll turkey wings in mixture to coat. Reserve remaining seasoned flour. In large heavy pot or Dutch oven, melt butter. Brown turkey on all sides. Add onions, garlic and saute five minutes. Add broth, carrots, celery, bay leaf and rosemary. Cover and simmer for 2½ hours or until turkey is tender. Transfer wings to heated platter. Remove bay leaf. Add enough flour to reserved flour to measure ⅓ cup. Mix with cold water to form smooth paste. Add slowly to hot liquid, stirring constantly. Cook over medium heat about five minutes or until sauce has thickened slightly. Pour over turkey on platter. Serve over hot noodles, if desired.

Turkey in a Sack

Grease a brown paper sack inside with melted shortening (use a sack of the right size to fit your bird); also brush turkey with melted shortening and salt and pepper well. Make a dressing and add oysters or mushrooms and stuff your bird. Then put the turkey in the bag and twist the end and tie with a string. Set the sack

in a pan and bake in a moderately slow oven (325°), 25 minutes per pound for total roasting. When done, take out of oven and do not open sack for at least 20 minutes, as this lets the steam go into the bird. Then open and serve. You will have a lovely brown bird. The paper sack will not catch on fire.

Sweet and Sour Turkey

1 wild turkey, cut up
2 onions, cut up
1 garlic clove
1 bay leaf
2 whole cloves
½ teaspoon mustard seed
2 tablespoons cornstarch
¼ cup sugar
½ cup vinegar
2 teaspoons salt
10 peppercorns

Place turkey pieces in pot with 4 cups of water. Add onion, garlic, bay leaf, cloves, mustard, salt and peppercorns. Bring to a boil, reduce heat, and put the lid on the pot and simmer for 2 hours. Remove the turkey and strain the broth. Return broth to pot, add cornstarch, combined with sugar and vinegar. Cook, stirring constantly, until the sauce thickens. Add turkey and simmer for 15 minutes.

Barbecued Turkey

One stick butter or margarine
½ cup chopped green onions or chives
1 cup of broth
¼ cup lemon juice
1 tablespoon thyme and savory, mixed
3 tablespoons parsley

Cook onions until tender in butter, add other ingredients. Bring to a full boil. Cut turkey in pieces, and cover each piece of turkey with this mixture. Baste often on grill. Cook 45 to 55 minutes or until done. If rotisserie is used, it takes about one and one-half hours until done.

Oven Fried Turkey

For each pound of wild turkey, blend ¼ cup flour, 1 teaspoon paprika, ¾ teaspoon salt, 1/8 teaspoon pepper, and 1/8 teaspoon poultry seasoning (optional) in a paper bag. Shake turkey pieces, 2 or 3 at a time, in bag to coat evenly, brown in at least ½ inch layer of fat in a heavy skillet. Place golden-browned turkey pieces, one layer deep, in a shallow baking pan. For each 2 pounds of wild turkey, spoon a mixture of 2 tablespoons of melted butter and 2 tablespoons of broth or milk over the turkey. Continue the cooking in a moderate oven (350°) until the turkey is tender. Test with fork. If fork penetrates easily, turkey is done. Turn once to crisp evenly. During the cooking, broth or milk may be drizzled over the turkey if it appears dry.

Wild Turkey and Rice

1 wild turkey
1 whole apple
1 package dry onion soup mix
1½ cups uncooked rice
2 tablespoons butter
1 or 2 cans mushroom soup

Prepare the turkey for roasting. Quarter the apple and lay inside the turkey. This will cut out some of the wild taste. Place in a greased roaster, sprinkle the onion soup mix over the bird, place in oven and bake until about half done.

Wash the rice and plump up in a kettle on top of the stove. When the rice plumps up and the turkey is half done lift the bird from the roaster and spread the rice in the bottom of the roaster. Place the bird back in the roaster on top of rice. Pour the canned mushroom soup over the bird, cover and bake until tender. The salt in the onion soup will also salt the bird so be careful about salting. Watch the moisture. You will probably need to add water to keep the turkey from sticking.

Turkey Turnovers

Filling:
2 tablespoons finely chopped onion
1 tablespoon butter
⅓ cup thin gravy or broth from bones
1½ cups finely cut leftover turkey with some skin
¼ cup finely chopped celery
1 teaspoon salt
½ cup grated carrot

Saute onion and celery in butter until soft, about 5 minutes. Add remaining ingredients and stir lightly with a fork to mix well.

Biscuit Mix:
1 cup flour

2 teaspoons baking powder
¼ teaspoon salt
pinch of poultry seasoning
⅓ cup shortening
about ⅓ cup milk

Sift flour, measure and resift 3 times with the next 3 ingredients. Cut in shortening with pastry blender until consistency of rice. Add milk all at once and stir quickly with a fork until dough stiffens. Knead quickly on a lightly floured board 8 times.

Roll out to a 12-inch square, cut in four squares. Place ¼ of filling in center of each square. Moisten edge of square and fold over, pressing sides together to seal. Prick tops for steam vents. Brush tops with melted butter. Bake on a cookie sheet at 425° for 10 to 15 minutes, or until golden brown. Serve with hot mushroom sauce. Serves 4.

Escalloped Turkey

Make your favorite dressing. Butter a pan and put in a layer of coarsely chopped turkey. Cover with a layer of dressing. Repeat this process until the pan is full. The top layer should be dressing. Pour over the top the broth from meat fryings of chicken or beef.

Bake until onion and eggs in dressing are done; usually 30 minutes at 350° oven will give a delightfully browned dressing. Any leftover ham may be mixed with the turkey if desired.

Wild Turkey Leftover Casserole

Use this recipe for leftover wild turkey or other game bird, either fried or baked:
2 large or 3 medium pieces of meat
2 tablespoons butter
¼ cup milk
½ green pepper, chopped
1 can mushroom soup, undiluted
dash of chopped red pepper or hot sauce

Remove skin from pieces of meat, strip meat from bones, and chop into small pieces. Place in 1½ quart to 2 quart baking dish. In a skillet, brown the chopped green pepper in butter, then add all ingredients except meat. Blend and bring to near boil. Pour over meat in baking dish and bake 25 or 30 minutes at 350°.

WOODCOCK

Woodcock must be plucked but should not be skinned. The skin will conserve moisture and flavor in the meat.

One woodock generally will serve one person.

Stuffed Woodcock

2 woodcocks, cleaned and wiped dry
salt and pepper
2 slices bacon
¼ cup crushed potato chips

Stuff cavities of birds with stuffing. Salt and pepper birds, roll in ¼ cup melted butter, then, in the crushed potato chips. Place in shallow baking dish, covering with bacon. Bake at 350 degrees for one hour or until fork tender. Garnish with paprika and a few toasted almond slices.

Dressing:
2 tablespoons butter
2 tablespoons chopped onion
2 tablespoons celery
⅔ cup fresh chopped mushrooms
¼ cup chopped toasted almonds
1/8 tablespoon salt
1/8 tablespoon pepper
2 teaspoons lemon juice

Saute onion, celery and mushrooms in butter. Add lemon juice and almonds, and salt and pepper. Stuff cavities of birds with dressing.

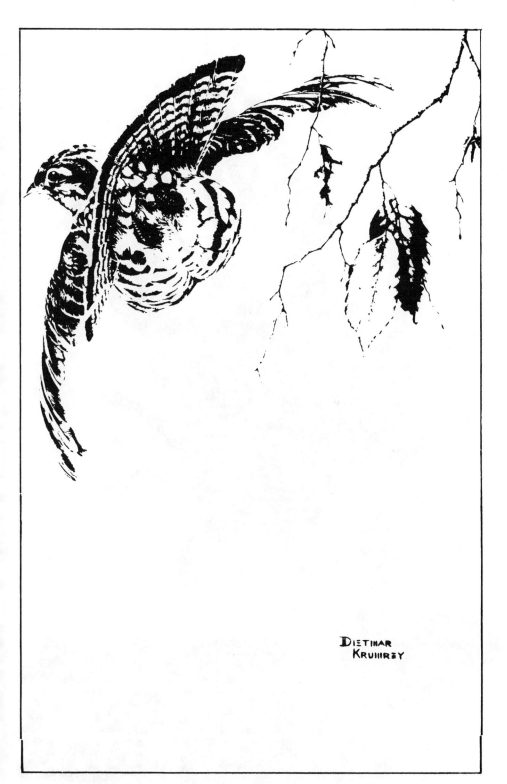

TURTLES, FROGS & CRAWDADS

TURTLE

Turn the freshly killed turtle on its back, taking care that it is dead and will not bite the handler. Cut off the head and let the blood drain at least 12 hours. Remove the flat lower shell by cutting with a sharp knife between the upper and lower shells. Cut out the meat, which must be cleaned of the gall and intestines, and lay aside such portions as are suitable for stews, ragouts, etc. Blanch to remove skin from the flippers and other parts. All turtle meat can be used for soups.

In making soups, cook the turtle only until the bones leave the flesh. Cooking it any longer will make the meat stringy.

Snapper is delicious when cut up in small pieces and cooked just like old-fashioned beef soup, with any assortment of vegetables desired.

Turtle Soup a la Creole

Cut the turtle meat into small pieces. Let it brown in a pot with a little lard. Cut up several onions, a slice of ham, and a little garlic, and stir and mix with turtle meat. Then let the mixture brown well.

Put in some flour and mix, pour a quantity of the soup stock into the pot, let it cool, and add a knee joint of veal.

Let it simmer for an hour, then put in some thyme, laurel leaf, parsley, shallots, and when everything is cooked, add more parsley and a couple slices of lemon chopped fine.

Just before serving add a wine glass full of Madeira wine or, in lieu of this, ⅔ that amount of lemon juice.

Turtle Soup Garnished with Quenelles

3 pounds turtle meat, cut small
4 tablespoons fat, ham or bacon drippings best
2 onions, minced
4 tablespoons flour, browned in fat
1 cup canned tomatoes
1 tablespoon salt
¼ clove garlic minced fine
2 bay leaves
2 sprigs parsley
6 cloves
2 blades mace (or ½ teaspoon mace)
1 lump sugar
2 tablespoons lemon juice
Parboil turtle meat 10 minutes. Save water to use as stock. Fry meat in fat. To 4 quarts of water and stock, add onions, flour, tomatoes, salt and garlic. Add turtle meat, bay leaves, parsley, cloves, mace, sugar and lemon juice. Cook for 3 hours, strain if desired.

Garnish soup with sliced hard cooked eggs or quenelles of turtle meat and a slice of lemon, cut thin and minced. Sherry jelly may be added for flavor.
Quenelles:

Put the turtle meat used in the soup through the meat grinder. For ½ pound of meat used, use ½ pound bread crumbs, 2 egg yolks, hard cooked. Season with salt, cayenne, parsley, thyme, cloves, mace. Add 2 whole eggs, 2 tablespoons lemon juice, and milk, water or stock to moisten. Roll and fry like croquettes and add to soup on serving.

Curry of Turtle

Take 1 pound of turtle meat, wash, cut into cubes, brown in fat with 1 large or 2 medium-sized onions. Put in pot 1 medium sized potato, 1 carrot, the onions which have been cooked with the turtle, a small piece of parsley, ½ teaspoon of pepper, 1 teaspoon of salt and ½ teaspoon of curry powder.

Add browned turtle meat to the mixture in the pot and let simmer until tender. Make molds by hollowing out cups of boiled rice and serve in the molds. This tastes like chicken or veal curry.

Steamed Turtle

Take fresh turtle meat, fill with black pepper and a bit of butter, steam until the flesh separates from the bones, then add black sauce (the soy bean sauce to be found in Chinese restaurants) or Worcestershire sauce.

Stewed Terrapin with Cream

2 tablespoons butter
1 tablespoon rice flour
1 pint thin cream
pinch cayenne
4 egg yolks
1 tablespoon salt
½ tablespoon white pepper
¼ tablespoon grated nutmeg
1 pint terrapin meat
1 tablespoon lemon juice

Place butter and rice flour in saucepan, stir over fire until it bubbles. Stir in 1 pint thin cream, salt, white pepper, nutmeg, cayenne, then the terrapin meat. Stir it all until scalding hot. Move saucepan to back part of stove where contents will keep hot, but not boil. Then stir in 4 well-beaten egg yolks. Do not boil, but pour immediately into a tureen containing 1 tablespoon lemon juice.

Serve hot.

Turtle Soup, New Jersey Style

Boil meat until well-cooked. Take out of broth, chop into small pieces and let cool.

Boil potatoes, onions and macaroni or spaghetti, the latter broken into 1'' pieces, in the broth. Do not add meat until onions, potatoes and spaghetti are well cooked.

Then add meat and chopped hard boiled egg. Add about 1 pint of milk to each quart of soup and 1 large tablespoon of butter.

As quantity of potatoes, onions, eggs, spaghetti, etc., must be gauged by the size of the turtle, no specific quantities can be given, but for an ordinary turtle, weighing about 8 pounds, the following proportions will be found proper:
2 medium size onions
6 medium size potatoes (diced)
2 20-minute boiled eggs

Soup may be thickened with flour and water. Salt and pepper to taste. Small quantity of wine or sherry, added before serving, will improve the flavor considerably.

Turtle Rivola

½ pound turtle meat, chopped in food grinder
2 onions
¼ pound cheese
salt and pepper
1 cup flour
1 egg
¼ teaspoon salt
butter

Cook turtle meat until tender with onions, add cheese, salt and pepper. Make a pasta with flour, egg, salt. Make a thick batter, roll out thin into a sheet of noodle dough, and cut into 2'' dice.

Take 1 spoonful of minced turtle meat, lay on the diced noodle dough, fold over 3 corners and enclose the meat, cook like noodles in the water that the turtle meat was cooked in, to which a spoonful of butter has been added.

FROGS

The younger and smaller a frog is, the sweeter and more tender its meat will be.

Cut off the frog's head and feet. The skin will slip right off. Remove the internal organs and wash the meat in cold water. Strip the white cord from each leg to keep it from jumping in response to the heat of the skillet.

Both the front and back legs of the frog are good to eat.

Fried Frog Legs

Frog legs can be simply fried in margarine or butter until tender.

Or they can be dipped in egg, then rolled in cracker crumbs or cornmeal before pan frying.

Another way to fry frog legs is to sprinkle them with salt, pepper and paprika, then roll them in cracker crumbs. Dip them in egg, and roll them in the crumbs again. Fry in deep fat at 375° F for 3 minutes or until golden brown. Drain and serve immediately. The paprika makes the meat take on a prettier golden brown color as it fries and does not affect the flavor.

Frog Legs a la Newburg

Boil together for 3 minutes 2 tablespoons butter, ½ cup Madeira salt and cayenne. Add 3 egg yolks and ½ pint cream, slightly beaten. Cook 2 minutes, stirring constantly. Pour over fried froglegs.

 # CRAWDADS OR CRAYFISH

Crawdads can be found in any shallow, unpolluted water. They can be caught with traps, a baited line, or by hand. Besides being good bait, they make excellent eating. If a crawdad drops its front claw when you grab for it, keep it. It contains some tender, delicious meat. The crawdad will regenerate a new claw.

To transport crawdads, put them in a bucket with some cool water. A dozen crawdads will feed one person.

Boiled Crawdads

Wash the crawdads in clean water. Some people soak them for 24 hours in fresh water. Throw out any which are dead before cooking. Bring a large pot of water to a boil with a few peppercorns and a bay leaf. Drop the crawdads in and boil 6 to 10 minutes. They will turn a bright red.

When the crawdads are cool, they are ready to eat. Twist off the head and discard it. Suck out the juices from the body. Break off the tail and shell it; it contains a lot of meat. Crack the claws and eat that meat, too.

Dip the tails and claws in lemon butter or shrimp sauce for a tasty treat.

Boiled crawdad tails can be used just like shrimp.

Crawdad Pie

Serves 8-10
about 4 dozen large crawdads
4 eggs
1 cup diced celery
1 cup grated sharp cheese
1½ cups mayonnaise
1½ tablespoons Worcestershire sauce
3 tablespoons sherry
buttered bread crumbs

Boil and shell crawdads and chop the meat. Beat eggs until frothy. Add crawdads and the other ingredients except bread crumbs. Put the mixture in a casserole dish and top with the bread crumbs. Bake at 325 degrees F for one hour. Can be served warm or refrigerated for later use.

Bob Gwizdz

SAUCES & STUFFINGS

SAUCES

Barbecue Sauce

1 quart ginger ale
1 bottle hot ketchup
1 bottle ketchup
¼ cup butter
2 tablespoons Worcestershire sauce
2 tablespoons steak sauce
½ cup brown sugar

Combine all ingredients. Bring to a boil, then turn down the heat and simmer for 35 minutes.

Cumberland Sauce

1 tablespoon sugar
1 egg yolk
¾ teaspoon dry mustard
2 tablespoons lemon juice
salt
pepper
8 ounces currant jelly
¼ cup raisins

Heat jelly in a double boiler until soft. Beat in first six ingredients. Cook 15 minutes, until thickened, stirring constantly. Add raisins. Serve with roast.

Game Sauce

Combine 6 tablespoons orange juice concentrate with half a cup each of ketchup, sherry and currant jelly. Beat, then let stand for a day in the refrigerator. Serve it warm or cold with game birds or venison.

Tartar Sauce

Combine:
1 cup mayonnaise or salad dressing
1 teaspoon onion juice or 1 tablespoon minced onion
1 tablespoon mixed capers
4 tablespoons finely chopped pickle or pickle relish
1 tablespoon minced parsley
1 tablespoon minced olives

Chill. Serve cold with fish. Serves 8 to 10.

Cranberry Tartar Sauce

Combine:
1 cup mayonnaise or salad dressing
½ cup jellied cranberry sauce
2 tablespoons chopped onion
¼ cup sweet pickle relish
2 tablespoons chopped olives (optional)
2 tablespoons chopped parsley
Chill. Serve with fish. Serves 12.

Lemon Butter Sauce

Melt ½ cup butter or margarine. Add the juice of one lemon, ½ teaspoon grated lemon rind, ½ teaspoon chopped chives, ½ teaspoon salt and 1/8 teaspoon white pepper. Simmer 3 minutes. Serve hot with fish. Serves 6-8.

Pineapple Sauce

Heat contents of one 20-ounce can of pineapple chunks. Dissolve 2 teaspoons cornstarch in ¼ cup cold water. Gradually add cornstarch to pineapple. Cook, stirring constantly until thickened. Serve warm with fish. Makes 16-20 servings.

Port Wine Sauce

½ glass currant jelly
½ glass port wine
½ glass stock
few grains red pepper
½ teaspoon salt
2 teaspoons lemon juice
4 cloves
Simmer the cloves and stock together for 30 minutes. Strain on the other ingredients and melt them together. Serve with game birds.

Barbecue Sauce for Dieters

1 cup tomato puree
¾ cup water
4 tablespoons minced onion
3 tablespoons vinegar
1 teaspoon salt
1 teaspoon paprika
1 teaspoon chili powder
½ teaspoon black pepper
3 tablespoons brown sugar
2 tablespoons Worcestershire sauce
¼ teaspoon cinnamon
1/8 teaspoon cloves
Combine all ingredients. Heat to boiling and boil one minute.

STUFFING

Stuffing can either be baked with fish or meat or simply baked in a casserole and served as a side dish.

Cheese Stuffing

½ cup sliced onion
¼ cup butter or margarine
2 tablespoons chopped parsley
1 cup grated Cheddar or Parmesan cheese
¾ teaspoon salt
dash pepper
2 cups dry bread crumbs
Saute onion in butter until tender. Add to remaining ingredients and mix thoroughly. Will stuff a 3 to 5 pound fish.

Sour Cream Stuffing

½ cup chopped onion
¼ cup melted butter or salad oil
¼ cup diced peeled lemon
1 quart dry bread crumbs
1 teaspoon paprika
¾ cup chopped celery
2 tablespoons grated lemon rind
½ cup sour cream
1 teaspoon salt
Saute onion and celery in butter. Mix lemon rind, sour cream, paprika and salt with bread crumbs. Add onion and celery and mix well. Enough for a 3 to 5 pound fish.

Whole Wheat Surprise Stuffing

1 cup chopped celery
2 small onions, finely chopped
½ pound sliced mushrooms
2 teaspoons poultry seasoning
1/8 teaspoon pepper
1 cup chopped celery leaves
¼ cup butter or margarine
1 loaf whole wheat bread crumbs
1 teaspoon salt
1 8 ounce bottle stuffed olives, chopped
Saute celery, leaves and onions in butter until onion becomes transluscent. Add mushrooms and cook 5 minutes longer. Combine with crumbs; add seasonings and olives. Place stuffing on one side of fish fillet; place other fillet on top and sew fish together. Lay fish on greased baking sheet and bake at 425 degrees F, allowing 10 minutes per pound. Baste frequently.

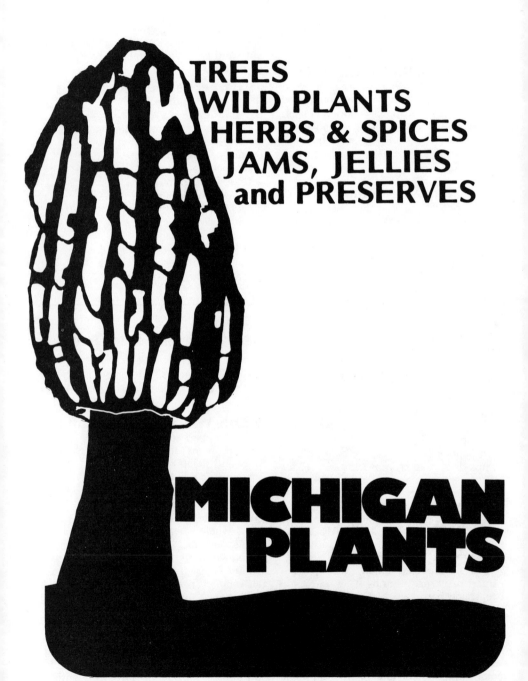

TREES
WILD PLANTS
HERBS & SPICES
JAMS, JELLIES
and PRESERVES

MICHIGAN
PLANTS

MORELS

May in Michigan means morels for hundreds of avid mushroom hunters. Morels pop up in any number of habitats throughout Michigan, and are especially thick when the spring is warm and rainy.

TYPES. Michigan has four types of morels. The black, the small white and the large white morels are distinguished by their brown to cream color and their pitted, cone-shaped caps attached to the stalk. These three types are edible.

The fourth type is the "false" morel. It appears in about the same places and at the same time as the others. The "false" morel contains a toxin which is usually destroyed in cooking, but which can cause a strong reaction if eaten. The "false" morel can be distinguished from the others by its wrinkled or wavy cap. The cap is not attached to the stalk; it may lie flat on the ground and can reach a weight of a quarter of a pound.

COLLECTING AND CLEANING. Collect morels in a basket or a paper sack. Morels stored in a plastic bag will spoil quickly.

Slice each mushroom in half lengthwise and wash carefully in running water to rinse out sand and bugs. Soak them for several hours in salt water, then drain.

FREEZING. Pack your mushrooms loosely in a plastic bag after rinsing and draining them. Eat them within three months of freezing them.

DRYING. Morels can be dried in the sun to preserve them. You can set them in the sun for a few days and pack them into airtight jars for later use. Or string them together lengthwise with a needle and thread and hang them in the kitchen. For about three weeks, you'll have dried morels just waiting to be cut off the string and used. Soaking them in hot water for a few minutes will replace the moisture the mushrooms have lost. Drying does not affect the morel's flavor.

USES. Morels are scrumptious with meat, in gravy or casseroles, or just plain.

Fry them in hot melted butter for a tender, flavorful treat. They are mostly liquid and will shrink considerably in size, leaving a lot of juice in your frying pan. You may simmer the mushrooms gently until the liquid cooks down.

Some people like to dip morels in a batter of egg, milk and flour, then fry them in oil or deep fat until they're golden brown.

Brown rice and mushrooms make a delicious side dish. Prepare 1 cup of brown rice and set aside. Clean and slice 6 to 8 morels (or other mushrooms). Chop 2 shallots. Saute the mushrooms in butter, add the shallot and let simmer. Don't let the shallots get too brown. Add 2 soup spoons of sherry and let the liquid reduce. Mix the rice into the mushrooms. Season with salt and pepper.

POPCORN

Michigan farmers are major producers of popcorn, that favorite treat of nibblers. Popcorn pops because the tough kernel holds in moisture which turns to steam when heated. The steam pressure explodes the kernel to forty times its original size.

Keep your popcorn in airtight jars to keep the moisture in. If your popcorn isn't very "poppy," sprinkle a little water in the jar, put on the cap and let it stand a few hours. This replaces the moisture in the kernels.

Popcorn is good for dieters. There are only 55 calories in a cup, and it is full of vitamins and minerals.

Carmel Corn

4½ quarts popped corn (9 tablespoons unpopped)
1 cup butter
2 cups brown sugar
½ cup dark molasses
1 teaspoon salt
2 tablespoons water

In medium saucepan, melt butter. Add brown sugar, molasses, salt and water. Stirring constantly, apply medium heat until mixture boils. Boil to 290 degrees, the hard crack stage. Pour over popcorn, bake at 250 degrees F for 20 minutes. Cool.

 MAPLE SYRUP

To make maple syrup, sap can be collected from sugar maples, ash-leaved maples and red maples. Be patient in collecting sap—it takes thirty to forty gallons of it to make one gallon of maple syrup. Exposure to the sun can sour sap, so collect the sap from the buckets as often as possible and boil it down quickly. The temperature of the sap should reach 218 degrees F and it should boil a long time to reach the density of syrup.

Maple Sugar

For soft maple sugar, boil the sap to a higher temperature than for syrup. Then cool it to 100° F, stirring until it's a dull yellow. Pour it into molds and let it harden.

Hard maple sugar should be boiled to an even higher temperature than soft maple sugar. Cool it quickly, and when it starts to crystallize, pour it into molds.

Maple sugar can be substituted for sugar in any recipe.

Yogurt

3 cups powdered milk
6 cups water
3 tablespoons sugar (optional)
1 large can evaporated milk
3 tablespoons yogurt
½ teaspoon unflavored gelatin

Soften gelatin in small bowl. Add enough boiling water to make one cup liquid. Dissolve in sugar (optional). Cool.

Preheat oven to 250 to 300°. Mix instant milk with 3 cups tepid water in big ceramic bowl. Add evaporated milk. Stir in 2 more cups lukewarm water and gelatin solution. Add a few drops vanilla flavoring if you want.

Thoroughly stir in 3 tablespoons yogurt. Cover bowl, put in oven. Turn oven to OFF. Remove from oven 8 to 10 hours later. Makes ½ gallon.

USES. Yogurt lends a refined taste to many other foods. Mix it with fresh fruit for a nutritious dessert. Top plain yogurt with fruit sauce, honey, preserves, nuts, sunflower seeds, coconut—anything!

Use yogurt in appetizer dips or as a dressing for salads. Fruit flavored yogurt is good as a topping for fruit salad. Put a spoonful of plain yogurt in canned soup for an enhanced flavor.

In baked goods, try using yogurt instead of milk. One-half teaspoon baking soda with each cup yogurt is equivalent in leavening power to one teaspoon baking powder with one cup milk.

Yogurt makes a good marinade for meat; spices blend into it easily. It can be your special secret for delicious sauces, gravies and stuffings.

Yogurt fills in for buttermilk in biscuits and pancakes when thinned with a little water.

Yogurt may be substituted for sour cream in most recipes, especially when calories are being counted and cooking isn't required. The finished product will be less rich and more tart.

WILD PLANT BEVERAGES _____

Dandelion Coffee
You can make a strong coffee from dandelion roots. Wash the roots well, then let them dry. When they're almost black, cut them into small pieces and grind them, (you could use two stones for the grinding process). Use the ground roots as coffee, one teaspoon per cup, or mix them with regular coffee.

Sassafras Tea
Cut sassafras roots into small pieces and boil them to make tea. Boil with sugar or maple syrup if you want a sweeter drink.

Wintergreen Tea
Wintergreen is a low shrub with creeping stems and shiny leaves on reddish branches. For tea, pour boiling water over the whole plant. Steep for 15 minutes.

Sumac Lemonade
The fruit of the staghorn sumac makes a drink that tastes like lemonade. Boil the fruit in water to the desired strength, then strain the liquid and add sweetener.

Chicory Coffee
Chicory roots are used today to give coffee a deeper color and to complement the flavor. Dry the roots, then roast and grind them. Use ground chicory just like coffee, or add it to your regular coffee.

 WILD SEASONING

Wild Mint
The mint plant has a square stem, opposite simple leaves, and small white, purple or pink flowers. The plant also gives off a minty aroma.

Add mint leaves to any recipe, or eat them raw, with salt, or in salads.

Wintergreen
Wintergreen is a low shrub with creeping stems, shiny leaves on reddish branches and bright red fruit. You can use any part of the plant as a spice.

Vinegar
Let the sap from a sugar maple or birch tree ferment in the sun. Strain it through a cloth.

Mustard
Mustard is an annual plant which has yellow flowers, big and lobed lower leaves, and small, toothed upper leaves. It can reach a height of five to six feet. Dry mustard seeds, then pound them and use like regular mustard.

Ginger
Wild ginger, or Canada snakeroot, grows in shady woods and bears purple and brown flowers and heart-shaped leaves. Sometimes these ground-hugging flowers are hidden by the leaves.

Boil the flowers or roots until the water smells strongly of ginger. Put it in the sun, where it will evaporate to a powder. Use the powder like regular ginger but double the amount since it is not as strong as that you buy.

JAMS, JELLIES AND PRESERVES

Jam, jelly and preserves are all fruit preserved by means of sugar and usually all are jellied to some extent. They are a good way to use fruit not at its best for canning or freezing—the largest and smallest fruits and those that are irregularly shaped.

Jelly is made from fruit juice; it is clear and firm enough to hold its shape when turned out of the container. Jam, made from crushed or ground fruit, tends to hold its shape but generally is less firm than jelly. Preserves are whole fruits or large pieces of fruit in a thick syrup, often slightly jellied.

Not all fruits have the properties needed for making satisfactory jellied products, but with the commercial pectins now available, you don't have to depend on the jellying quality of the fruit for successful results.

Apple Jelly
without added pectin

4 cups apple juice (about 3 pounds apples and 3 cups water)
2 tablespoons strained lemon juice, if desired
3 cups sugar

To prepare juice. Select about one-fourth underripe and three-fourths fully ripe tart apples. (Sort, wash and remove stem and blossom ends.) Do not pare or core. Cut apples into small pieces. Add water, cover and bring to boil on high heat. Reduce heat and simmer for 20 to 25 minutes, or until apples are soft. Extract juice.

To make jelly. Measure apple juice into a kettle. Add lemon juice and sugar and stir well. Boil over high heat to 8° F. above the boiling point of water, or until jelly mixture sheets from a spoon.

Remove from heat; skim off foam quickly. Pour jelly immediately into hot containers and seal.

Makes 4 or 5 eight-ounce glasses.

Blackberry Jelly
with powdered pectin

3½ cups blackberry juice (about 3 quart boxes berries)
1 package powdered pectin
4½ cups sugar

To prepare juice. Sort and wash fully ripe berries; remove any stems or caps. Crush berries and extract juice.

To make jelly. Measure juice into kettle. Add pectin and stir well. Place on high heat and, stirring constantly, bring quickly to a full rolling boil that cannot be stirred down.

Add sugar, continue stirring, and heat again to a full rolling boil. Boil hard for 1 minute.

Remove from heat; skim off foam quickly. Pour jelly immediately into hot containers and seal.

Makes 5 or 6 eight-ounce glasses.

Strawberry Jelly

Select fully ripe sound strawberries. About 3 quart boxes are needed for each batch of jelly. Sort the berries. Wash about 1 quart at a time by placing berries in a wire basket and moving the basket up and down several times in cold water. Drain the berries.

Remove caps and crush the berries. Place crushed berries, a small amount at a time, in a damp jelly bag or double thickness of cheesecloth held in a colander over a bowl.

Bring the edges of the cloth together and twist tightly. Press or squeeze to extract the juice. Strain the juice again through two thicknesses of damp cheesecloth without squeezing.

Measure 4 cups of juice into a large kettle. Add 7½ cups of sugar to the juice; stir to dissolve the sugar.

Place the kettle over high heat and, stirring constantly, bring the mixture quickly to a full rolling boil that cannot be stirred down.

Add 1 bottle of liquid pectin. Again, bring to a full rolling boil and boil hard for 1 minute.

Remove from heat and skim off foam quickly. If allowed to stand, the jelly may start to "set" in the kettle.

Pour jelly immediately into hot glasses to ½ inch of top. Cover each glass with a 1/8 inch layer of paraffin. Cool glasses on a metal rack or folded cloth, then cover with metal or paper lids, label and store in a cool, dry place.

Cherry Jelly
with powdered pectin

3½ cups cherry juice (about 3 pounds or 2

quart boxes sour cherries and ½ cup water)
1 package powdered pectin
4½ cups sugar

To prepare juice. Select fully ripe cherries. Sort, wash and remove stems; do not pit. Crush cherries, add water, cover, bring to boil on high heat. Reduce heat and simmer for 10 minutes. Extract juice.

To make jelly. Measure juice into a kettle. Add pectin and stir well. Place on high heat and, stirring constantly, bring quickly to a full rolling boil that cannot be stirred down.

Add sugar, continue stirring, and heat again to a full rolling boil. Boil hard for 1 minute.

Remove from heat; skim off foam quickly. Pour jelly immediately into hot containers and seal.

Makes about 6 eight-ounce glasses.

Grape Jelly
with liquid pectin

4 cups grape juice (about 3½ pounds Concord grapes and ½ cup water)
7 cups sugar
½ bottle liquid pectin

To prepare juice. Sort, wash and remove stems from fully ripe grapes. Crush grapes, add water, cover and bring to boil on high heat. Reduce heat and simmer for 10 minutes. Extract juice.

To prevent formation of tartrate crystals in the jelly, let juice stand in a cool place overnight, then strain through two thicknesses of damp cheesecloth to remove crystals.

To make jelly. Measure juice into a kettle. Stir in sugar. Place on high heat and, stirring constantly, bring quickly to a full rolling boil that cannot be stirred down.

Add pectin and heat again to a full rolling boil. Boil hard for 1 minute.

Remove from heat; skim off foam quickly. Pour jelly immediately into hot containers and seal.

Makes 8 or 9 eight-ounce glasses.

Wild Crabapple Jelly
without added pectin

4 cups crabapple juice (about 3 pounds crabapples and 3 cups water)
4 cups sugar

To prepare juice. Select firm, crisp

crabapples, about one-fourth underripe and three-fourths fully ripe. Sort, wash, and remove stem and blossom ends; do not pare or core. Cut crabapples into small pieces. Add water, cover, and bring to boil on high heat. Reduce heat and simmer for 20 to 25 minutes, or until crabapples are soft. Extract juice.

To make jelly. Measure juice into a kettle. Add sugar and stir well. Boil over high heat to 8° F. above the boiling point of water, or until mixture sheets from a spoon.

Remove from heat; skim off foam quickly. Pour jelly immediately into hot containers and seal. Makes 4 or 5 8 ounce glasses.

Wild Mint Jelly
with liquid pectin

1 cup chopped mint leaves and tender stems
1 cup water
½ cup cider vinegar
3½ cups sugar
5 drops green food coloring
½ bottle liquid pectin.

To prepare mint. Wash and chop mint. Pack solidly in a cup.

To make jelly. Measure mint into a kettle. Add vinegar, water, and sugar; stir well. Place on high heat and, stirring constantly, bring quickly to a full rolling boil that cannot be stirred down.

Add food coloring and pectin; heat again to a full rolling boil. Boil hard for ½ minute.

Remove from heat. Skim. Strain through two thicknesses of damp cheesecloth. Pour jelly immediately into hot containers and seal.

Makes 3 or 4 eight-ounce glasses.

Plum Jelly
with liquid pectin

4 cups plum juice (about 4½ pounds plums and ½ cup water)
7½ cups sugar
½ bottle liquid pectin

To prepare juice. Sort and wash fully ripe plums and cut in pieces; do not peel or pit. Crush fruit, add water, cover and bring to boil over high heat. Reduce heat and simmer for 10 minutes. Extract juice.

To make jelly. Measure juice into a kettle. Stir in sugar. Place on high heat and, stirring constantly, bring quickly to a full rolling boil that cannot be stirred down.

Add pectin; bring again to full rolling boil. Boil hard 1 minute.

Remove from heat; skim off foam quickly. Pour jelly immediately into hot containers and seal.

Makes 7 or 8 eight-ounce glasses.

Blackberry Jam with powdered pectin

6 cups crushed blackberries (about 3 quart boxes berries)
1 package powdered pectin
8½ cups sugar

To prepare fruit. Sort and wash fully ripe berries; remove any stems or caps. Crush berries. If they are very seedy, put part or all of them through a sieve or food mill.

To make jam. Measure crushed berries into a kettle. Add pectin and stir well. Place on high heat and, stirring constantly, bring quickly to a full boil with bubbles over the entire surface.

Add sugar, continue stirring, and heat again to a full bubbling boil. Boil hard for 1 minute, stirring constantly. Remove from heat; skim.

Fill and seal containers.

Process 5 minutes in boiling water bath.

Makes 11 or 12 half-pint jars.

Peach Jam

Sort and wash fully ripe peaches. Remove stems, skins and pits.

Crush or chop the peaches. A stainless steel potato masher is useful for this purpose.

Measure 3¾ cups of crushed peaches into a large kettle.

Add one package of powdered pectin and ¼ cup of lemon juice. Stir well to dissolve the pectin. Place on high heat and, stirring constantly, bring quickly to a full boil with bubbles over the entire surface.

Stir in 5 cups of sugar, continue stirring, and heat again to a full bubbling boil. Boil hard for 1 minute, stirring constantly to prevent sticking.

Remove jam from heat and skim and stir alternately for 5 minutes to help prevent fruit from floating.

Pour the jam into hot canning jars to 1/8 inch from top. Place clean, hot metal lid on, with sealing compound next to glass. Screw metal band down tight. Process 5 minutes in boiling water bath. Cool jars on a metal rack or folded cloth, then label and store in a cool, dry place.

Cherry Jam with powdered pectin

4 cups ground or finely chopped pitted cherries (about 3 pounds or 2 quart boxes sour cherries)
1 package powdered pectin
5 cups sugar

To prepare fruit. Sort and wash fully ripe cherries; remove stems and pits. Grind cherries or chop fine.

To make jam. Measure prepared cherries into a kettle. Add pectin and stir well. Place on high heat and, stirring constantly, bring quickly to a full boil with bubbles over the entire surface.

Add sugar, continue stirring, and heat again to a full bubbling boil. Boil hard for 1 minute, stirring constantly. Remove from heat; skim.

Fill and seal containers.

Process 5 minutes in boiling water bath.

Makes 6 half-pint jars.

Rhubarb-Strawberry Jam with liquid pectin

1 cup cooked red-stalked rhubarb (about 1 pound rhubarb and ¼ cup water)
2½ cups crushed strawberries (about 1½ quart boxes)
6½ cups sugar
½ bottle liquid pectin

To prepare fruit. Wash rhubarb and slice thin or chop; do not peel. Add water, cover, and simmer until rhubarb is tender (about 1 minute).

Sort and wash fully ripe strawberries; remove stems and caps. Crush berries.

To make jam. Measure prepared rhubarb and strawberries into a kettle. Add sugar and stir well. Place on high heat and, stirring constantly, bring quickly to a full boil with bubbles over the entire surface. Boil hard for 1 minute, stirring constantly.

Remove from heat and stir in pectin. Skim.

Fill and seal containers.

Process 5 minutes in boiling water bath.

Makes 7 or 8 half-pint jars.

Spiced Blueberry-Peach Jam
without added pectin

4 cups chopped or ground peaches (about 4 pounds peaches)
4 cups blueberries (about 1 quart fresh blueberries or 2 10-ounce packages of unsweetened frozen blueberries)
2 tablespoons lemon juice
½ cup water
5½ cups sugar
½ teaspoon salt
1 stick cinnamon
½ teaspoon whole cloves
¼ teaspoon whole allspice

To prepare fruit. Sort and wash fully ripe peaches; peel and remove pits. Chop or grind peaches.

Sort, wash and remove any stems from fresh blueberries. Thaw frozen berries.

To make jam. Measure fruits into a kettle; add lemon juice and water. Cover, bring to a boil, and simmer for 10 minutes, stirring occasionally.

Add sugar and salt; stir well. Add spices tied in cheesecloth. Boil rapidly, stirring constantly, to 9°F. above the boiling point of water, or until the mixture thickens.

Remove from heat; take out spices. Skim.
Fill and seal containers.
Process 5 minutes in boiling water bath.
Makes 6 or 7 half-pint jars.

Uncooked Berry Jam
with powdered pectin

2 cups crushed strawberries or black-berries (about 1 quart berries)
4 cups sugar
1 package powdered pectin
1 cup water

To prepare fruit. Sort and wash fully ripe berries. Drain. Remove caps and stems; crush berries.

To make jam. Place prepared berries in a large mixing bowl. Add sugar, mix well, and let stand for 20 minutes, stirring occasionally.

Dissolve pectin in water and boil for 1 minute. Add pectin solution to berry-and-sugar mixture; stir for 2 minutes.

Pour jam into freezer containers or canning jars, leaving ½ inch space at the top. Cover containers and let stand at room temperature for 24 hours or until jam has set.

Makes 5 or 6 half-pint jars.

To store. Store uncooked jams in refrigerator or freezer. They can be held up to 3 weeks in a refrigerator or up to a year in a freezer. If kept at room temperature they will mold or ferment in a short time. Once a container is opened, jam should be stored in the refrigerator and used within a few days.

NOTE: If jam is too firm, stir to soften. If it tends to separate, stir to blend. If it is too soft, bring it to a boil. It will thicken on cooling.

BREADS & DESSERTS

Hush Puppies

Mix 2 cups cornmeal, 1 cup milk or water, 1 teaspoon salt, 2 teaspoons baking powder and 1 finely diced onion. Shape into balls. Fry in the fat that you fried your fish in, and serve with fish for a special treat.

Sourdough

For best results use glass or pottery containers to keep the starter in. A good starter contains only flour, water and yeast. The liquid will separate from the batter when it stands several days, but this does not matter. If replenished every few days with flour and more water, the starter keeps fresh. If starter is not to be used for several weeks, freeze or dry it to keep it from spoiling. To carry it to camp, add enough flour to shape it into a ball and place it in a sack of flour. In the dried form the yeast goes in to a spore stage which will keep inert for a long time. Water and warmth bring the yeast back to the active stage.

2 cups flour
1 package dry yeast or 1 yeast cake
2 cups warm water

Mix these well. Place in warm place or closed cupboard overnight. In the morning put ½ cup of the starter in a scalded pint jar with a tight cover and store in the refrigerator or a cool place for future use. This is sourdough starter. The remaining batter can be used for pancakes, waffles, muffins, bread, or cake immediately. Add soda to the batter to make it light. If too much is added, the product is brownish when baked. If too little soda is used, the product tastes sour. Add soda just before baking, to one tablespoon of the liquid. Add this to the batter last, mix thoroughly, and bake. Don't add soda to the starter, as it kills the yeast.

Cheese Bread

1 egg
3¾ cups Bisquick
1½ cups milk
1 cup grated Cheddar cheese

Beat eggs and add milk. Stir in Bisquick and cheese. Beat 30 seconds, or until blended. (Dough will be lumpy). Pour into greased 9 x 5 x 3'' loaf pan. Bake in preheated moderate oven 1 hour. Slice ½ inch thick and serve hot.

Variations: **Cheese-Bacon Bread**—to above dough, add ⅓ cup bacon bits. **Chili-Cheese Bread**—to above dough, add ¾ teaspoon chili powder.

Makes 1 loaf bread.

Johnny Cake

1 cup cornmeal
½ cup sugar
4 tablespoons melted butter
1 cup flour
1 level teaspoon soda
1 cup sour milk or buttermilk

Mix liquid ingredients. Add the rest. Bake at 350°.

Onion Bread

1 cup milk, scalded (or use potato water)
3 tablespoons sugar
¾ cup warm water
1 envelope onion soup mix
1½ tablespoons butter
1 package active dry yeast
4 cups unsifted all purpose flour

In medium bowl, mix milk, sugar, butter. Cool to lukewarm. Sprinkle yeast in warm water. Stir until dissolved. Add yeast mixture to milk mixture. Add soup mix and flour. Stir and blend 2 minutes. Cover and let rise in warm place until double in size (about 45 minutes). Beat down and knead. Shape into 2 loaves. Let rise until doubled again. Bake in 350° oven for ½ hour. Makes 2 loaves.

Gladys Eggleton • Ann Arbor, MI

Sourdough Hotcakes

Sourdough hotcakes are leavened with a yeast starter and soda. The starter must be set the night before it is to be used. The starter, replenished every week with flour and water, will last weeks. Set the sponge for sourdough hotcakes the night before your breakfast. Place the starter in a medium size mixing bowl. Add 2 cups warm water and 2 cups flour. Beat well and set in a warm place, free from draft, to develop overnight. In the morning the batter will have gained ½ again its bulk and be covered with air bubbles. It will have a pleasant yeasty odor.

To make sourdough hotcakes for three persons, set aside ½ cup of the sponge in the refrigerator jar for your sourdough starter for next time. To remaining sponge add:

1 or 2 eggs
1 teaspoon soda
1 teaspoon salt
1 tablespoon sugar

Beat with a fork and blend in all ingredients. Add 2 tablespoons melted fat. Bake on a hot griddle. Turn once. Serve with a mixture of hot brown-sugar syrup, or honey and melted butter. Molasses, jelly or rose hip syrup are other tasty combinations.

Sourdough Bread

Set sponge as for sourdough hotcakes and let stand in a warm place overnight or for 6-8 hours. Save ½ cup for next starter. To the remaining sponge, which should be about 2 cups add:

4 cups sifted flour (or more)
2 tablespoons sugar
1 teaspoon salt
2 tablespoons fat
(¼ teaspoon soda added later)

Sift dry ingredients in a bowl, making a well in the center. Add fat to the sponge and mix well. Pour into the well of flour. Add enough flour to make a soft dough for kneading. Knead on a floured board for 10-15 minutes. Place in a greased bowl. Cover with a towel and let rise in a warm place for 2-4 hours or until doubled. Dissolve the ¼ teaspoon of soda in a tablespoon of warm water and add to the dough. Knead it in thoroughly. Shape dough into loaves in bread pans and set aside to rise. When doubled, bake at 375 degrees F for 50 to 60 minutes.

Springerle Cookies

4 large eggs
3-4 cups sifted flour
pinch of salt
1 pound powdered sugar
1 level teaspoon baking powder

Beat eggs until light, add sugar and salt. Beat for 3 minutes. Add flour until quite stiff. Divide into 4 sections. Roll out and press with floured board to make figures. Cut apart and lay out on cloth to dry overnight. Put anise seeds on bottom of each cookie. Bake 15-20 minutes at 325° until light color. Makes about 90 cookies.

Mrs. Crowe • Kalamazoo, MI

Apple Cookies

1 cup lard or oleo, creamed
4 eggs well beaten
2 cups chopped apples, peeled
3½ cups flour
1 teaspoon cinnamon
1 teaspoon soda
½ teaspoon nutmeg
1½ cups oatmeal
2 cups brown sugar
1 cup raisins
½ teaspoon salt

Cream lard or oleo, add sugar and beat. Add eggs and mix sifted flour with spices, soda, salt and oatmeal. Add to creamed mixture. Add chopped apples and raisins. Mix well. Drop on greased cookie sheet and bake at 350°

Shoo Fly Pie

Bottom part: Mix together ¾ cup molasses or corn syrup, ¾ cup boiling water, ½ teaspoon soda (1/8 teaspoon each may be added of nutmeg, cloves, cinnamon and ginger).

Top part: Crumb; 1½ cups flour, ¼ cup shortening, ½ cup brown sugar.

Pastry: Make one 9'' pie crust. Add a layer of crumbs in crust. Add ⅓ of the liquid mixture, then another layer of crumbs, and continue to alternate layers ending with a layer of crumbs on top. Bake at 375° for 35 minutes.

Keep-Long Oatmeal Cake

1½ cups boiling water
½ cup butter or margarine
1 teaspoon cinnamon
1 cup quick-cooking oats
2 eggs
1 teaspoon nutmeg

1 cup white sugar
1½ cups flour
½ teaspoon salt
1 cup brown sugar
1 teaspoon soda
½ cup raisins or chopped nuts

Pour boiling water over oats. Mix well. Cream butter and sugars thoroughly. Beat in eggs. Stir in soaked oatmeal. Stir dry ingredients into the oatmeal mixture, add raisins or nuts (if desired) and pour into a greased 13 x 9 x 2'' pan. Bake at 350° for 35 minutes or until done.

Cool in pan. Spread with topping:
¼ cup brown sugar
6 tablespoons butter
½ cup white sugar
¼ cup light cream
1 cup flaked coconut
¼ teaspoon vanilla
1 cup chopped nuts

Heat until bubbly. Stir in vanilla. Spread on top of cake and broil about 3 minutes. Do not cut cake for a day. Cake keeps very well for many days.

No-Egg Oatmeal Drops

½ cup butter
1 cup sweet milk
1 teaspoon vanilla
3 cups flour
1 cup shredded coconut
2 teaspoons baking powder
1 cup raisins
1½ cups sugar
1½ cups uncooked oatmeal
¼ teaspoon salt

Cream butter and sugar. Add milk and dry ingredients. Mix well. Add raisins, coconut, vanilla, oatmeal. Drop by the tablespoonfuls on a greased baking sheet, 1 inch apart. Bake in hot oven 5 minutes, then reduce heat to little below moderate until light golden brown.

Parmesan Popovers

3 eggs
2 tablespoons melted butter or margarine
½ teaspoon salt
1 cup milk
1 cup sifted all purpose flour
6 to 7 tablespoons Parmesan cheese

Beat eggs slightly; add milk and melted butter. Beat until blended. Gradually beat in flour and salt. Oil 5 6 oz., custard cups and arrange in a jelly-roll pan or on cookie sheet. Place 1 tablespoon grated Parme-

san cheese in each cup and pour batter into cups to within ¼ inch of top. Bake in preheated moderate oven (375°F) 60 minutes. Sprinkle top of each popover with 1 teaspoon grated Parmesan, then quickly cut slit in side of each to let out steam. Continue baking 10 to 15 minutes longer or until tops are firm, crisp and deep brown. Remove popovers from cups immediately, loosening with spatula, onto wire rack. Serve piping hot, with butter or margarine.

Makes 5 popovers.

French Rhubarb Pie

Mix together:
1 egg
1 teaspoon vanilla
2 tablespoons flour
1 cup sugar
2 cups diced rhubarb

Pour into unbaked pie shell. Cover with topping:
¾ cup flour
½ cup brown sugar
⅓ cup margarine

Bake at 400°F for 10 minutes. Bake at 350° for 30 minutes.

Strawberry Pie

1 9'' baked pie shell
3 tablespoons cornstarch
1 tablespoon lemon juice
1 tablespoon butter
1 quart strawberries, washed
½ cup cold water
¼ teaspoon salt
1 cup sugar

Put half of berries into shell. Crush the rest. Add other ingredients. Cook until thick. Add red food coloring. Cool. Pour over berries in pie shell. Refrigerate and top with whipped cream when ready to serve.

Ozark Pudding

1 egg
½ cup sugar
3 heaping tablespoons flour
1½ teaspoons baking powder
1/8 teaspoon salt
½ cup ground nuts
½ cup diced apples

Bake in 7'' pie pan at 350° for 25 minutes. Serve with ice cream or whipped cream.

Grandmother's Peach Cobbler

⅔ cup sugar
1 tablespoon cornstarch
1 cup water
3 cups fresh sliced peaches
1 teaspoon lemon
2 tablespoons butter
½ teaspoon cinnamon
1 cup sifted flour
1 tablespoon sugar
1½ teaspoons baking powder
½ teaspoon salt
3 tablespoons shortening
½ cup milk

Mix sugar and cornstarch in saucepan; gradually stir in water. Bring to boiling. Boil one minute, stirring constantly. Add peaches and lemon. Pour into 1½ quart baking dish. Sprinkle with cinnamon and dot with butter. Sift flour, sugar, baking powder, and salt into bowl. Cut in shortening until mixture resembles coarse crumbs. Stir in milk to make soft dough. Drop by spoonfuls onto fruit mixture. Bake at 400° 25 to 30 minutes. Serve warm with cream, whipped cream or ice cream. Serves 6 to 8.

Apple Crumb Pie

5 to 7 tart apples
1 cup sugar
¾ cup enriched flour
1 9" unbaked pie shell
1 teaspoon cinnamon
⅓ cup butter

Pare apples, cut in eighths, arrange in pie shell. Mix ½ cup sugar with cinnamon. Set aside. Mix ½ cup sugar with flour; cut in butter until crumbly. Sprinkle over apples. Bake in hot oven (400°) 40 minutes or until done. Cool. Spoon whipped cream on top and sprinkle with cinnamon sugar mixture.

My Grandma's Plum Pudding

Mix well:
1 cup suet, chopped fine
½ cup molasses
1 cup raisins
½ teaspoon nutmeg
½ cup nutmeats
1 cup sweet milk
2 cups flour
1 cup dates, chopped fine

1 teaspoon cinnamon
1 teaspoon soda

Wrap in double thickness of cheesecloth or white cloth. Steam for about 3 hours (if doubling recipe, 4-5 hours). Serve with warm sauce of:
1½ cup brown sugar
1 cup water
½ cup butter

Thicken with cornstarch to gravy consistency. Add rum flavoring to taste. Pudding should be served warm, topped with warm sauce and whipped cream.

Louise Senecal • Muskegon, MI

Apple Pudding Cake

Mix in large bowl:
2 cups sugar
½ cup chopped nuts
2 eggs, beaten
2 cups sliced apples
½ cup oil
½ cup raisins
1 teaspoon vanilla

Mix in another bowl:
2⅔ cups flour
½ teaspoon nutmeg
1 teaspoon baking powder
½ teaspoon cinnamon
1 teaspoon baking soda
1½ teaspoons salt

Add flour mixture to apple mixture. Mix well. Pour in greased 9" x 18" baking dish. Bake 1 hour at 350°.

Topping:
1½ cups cold milk
1 envelope Dream Whip
1 package vanilla instant pudding

Combine and beat 5 minutes with electric beater. When pudding is cool, frost with topping and chill several hours in refrigerator.

Cherry Chocolate Cake

1 cup shortening
2 eggs, beaten
3 cups flour
pinch of salt
2 squares melted chocolate
2 cups sugar
2 cups sour milk (2 cups milk plus 2 tablespoons lemon juice or vinegar)
2 teaspoons soda
6 tablespoons cherry juice
sweet cherries, slightly chopped

Mix shortening, eggs, flour, salt, sugar, milk and soda. Blend cherry juice with melted chocolate and add to batter. Stir in cherries. Bake in 9'' x 13'' pan for 60 minutes at 350°.

The cake will appear to have fallen when it cools from the oven but it will be scrumptious.

Strawberry Cake

1 package deluxe white cake mix
1 package strawberry Jello
½ cup vegetable oil
4 eggs
1 cup mashed or blended strawberries, frozen or fresh
½ cup vegetable oil

Mix all ingredients and beat 4 minutes until light and fluffy. Bake in greased floured tube pan at 350° for 1 hour. Use juice from strawberries to make confectioners sugar glaze.

Rhubarb Torte

Mix:
3 cups rhubarb (½'' cubes)
¼ cup all purpose flour
1 cup sugar
2 beaten eggs
Spread over bottom of 8 x 8 x 2'' pan.
Topping:
¾ cup flour
¼ cup shortening
¾ cup brown sugar

Blend until fine and spread over rhubarb. Bake at 350° for 45 minutes. Serve plain or with topping.

Apples can be substituted; with blueberries reduce sugar to ½ cup.

Apple Crisp

Fill bottom of buttered 8 x 12 inch glass casserole with sliced tart apples. (Wolf-River or Macintosh). Sprinkle with:
1 cup brown sugar
½ teaspoon cinnamon
Mix as for pie crust:
½ cup flour
½ teaspoon salt
½ cup oatmeal
½ cup butter
½ cup white sugar

Spread over apples. Bake at 350° until apples are done and top is brown. Your casserole can be half full of apples.

CAMP
COOKING

Start planning your camping trip weeks before you leave so you can be sure you bring only what you need— no more and no less. Isn't it worth a little planning time to make sure you don't forget any essential or lug around extra weight during your trip?

As a camp cook, you will have four areas of concern: Cooking and serving, storage and refrigeration, packing and transporting food and utensils, and the clean up detail. Here are some suggestions:

1. Keep a checklist of equipment you packed at home, and recheck it as you leave each site.

2. For cooking, most campers have three choices: a folding two or three burner stove which uses either propane, butane, or unleaded gasoline; a collapsible charcoal grill; or an open fire. Be sure you know how to start and control your fire. Make sure you have plenty of fuel.

3. For equipment, take along a 10-inch skillet with a cover, a set of sturdy nested pots with lids that double as small saucepans (sold at most sporting goods stores), and a large water bucket.

4. Heavy-duty aluminum foil is useful for both cooking and storing. Don't forget you can wash and reuse the foil.

5. Heavy-duty rectangular baskets and cardboard crates with hard holes, waterproofed with a coat of shellac, are best for transporting food and equipment.

6. Mark the contents of each box. Organize your gear so that you can get at the cooking utensils to start dinner while camp is being set up.

7. Keep your campsite clean. You don't want to attract any woodland animals.

8. Use an insulated ice chest with a tight-fitting cover. Remember to drain the chest daily to prevent water damage to the food. Check the ice supply before settling down for the night.

9. Have a pan of soapy dishwater handy while cooking to clean your utensils as they're used. Put the final dishwater on to heat as you eat dinner.

10. Don't let garbage collect. Either put garbage in a sealed bag or bury it. Even soapy dishwater contains particles of food, so dig a small ditch away from your site, dump your dishwater, and cover with dirt.

Here are some campfire guidelines:

1. Make sure your chosen area is clean of flammable materials and is not close to a tree, bush, or exposed roots.

2. Collect rocks to place in a circle around the fire. Don't get them from lakes or streams because the absorbed water can make a rock explode when it gets hot.

3. Gather kindling and group it in three piles: small twigs, thumb-size sticks, and larger pieces. Make sure the wood is dry and not rotten.

4. Before bedding down, collect enough wood for breakfast. You'll appreciate it in the morning.

5. Use tightly-wadded newspaper, bark, or forest sweepings as a base. Build a cone of small twigs over it. Add bigger pieces in teepee form.

6. Make sure your fire is well ventilated.

7. Allow at least an hour for your fire to build. The flames should die down and turn the embers to a smoky glow or your charcoal to a white-ash color before you start cooking.

8. Never leave your fire unattended.

Now, here are some recipes to try out on your camping trip. Some are for the fish or game you've just caught while hunting and that you just can't wait to eat. Enjoy!

BREAKFASTS

Bits of Pork Pancakes

½ pound pork sausage
1 cup small curd cottage cheese with chives
½ teaspoon salt
½ teaspoon caraway seeds
3 eggs
¼ cup rye flour

Break sausage into bits while browning; save grease. Beat eggs in separate bowl. Add sausage and all remaining ingredients, mixing well. Cook on a hot griddle, lightly greased with pork grease. Serve with applesauce or sour cream or both. 4 servings.

Straggler's Breakfast

1 egg
butter
Cheddar cheese, cubed
salt & pepper
1 large bread slice
ketchup
paprika
bacon

WIth rim of glass, cut a hole in the center of the bread. Butter both sides of the bread. Place on hot grill. Drop dot of butter into center; break egg into hole. Place cheese on top of egg and top with dash of ketchup. Sprinkle with paprika, salt and pepper. Place strips of bacon over top. Cover and cook to taste. Turn over for well done.

Scotch Eggs

4 medium size hard cooked eggs
1 teaspoon flour
3 ounces dry bread crumbs
12 ounces bulk breakfast sausage
1 beaten egg
salt and pepper to taste

Shell the eggs and dry them with paper towels. Mix the flour, salt and pepper. Mold the 3 ounces sausage around each egg, coating evenly. Dip each coated egg in beaten egg, then roll in crumbs. Deep fat fry until golden and thoroughly cooked, about 3 minutes.

When cool, wrap in foil and take along on your trip. The eggs are best when eaten cold.

New England Ham Fritters

⅔ cup sifted flour
⅓ cup milk
1 tablespoon mustard
½ cup crushed pineapple, well drained
1 teaspoon baking powder
2 eggs
2 cups cooked ground ham
fat

Put flour and baking powder in mixing bowl; add milk, eggs and mustard, mixing until smooth. Fold in ham and pineapple. Heat ½ inch fat to 350°. Drop ham mixture from a teaspoon into hot fat. Fry on one side until golden brown; turn and fry on other side. Drain on paper towl. 5-6 servings.

One Big Pancake

2 cups flour
3 teaspoons baking powder
¼ teaspoon salt
1 tablespoon egg powder
1¼ cup condensed milk
2 tablespoons melted butter

Mix first 5 ingredients in frying pan. Add milk and butter. Work the dough until it holds together. Put over medium heat for 15 minutes. This makes one big pancake to split among the campers or to eat alone if you're hungry! Experiment with the pancake. I throw raisins, corn, fruit, or almost anything edible into the batter for a new flavor.

Mike Brown • Norton Shores, MI

Cereal Crunch

2 cups wheat flakes
2 cups rye flakes
2 cups soy flakes
2 cups oatmeal
2 cups toasted wheat germ
2 cups raisins
2 cups chopped mixed nuts
brown sugar (optional)

Mix. For camping, add powdered milk to the mixture, then all you'll need is water when you're in the wilderness.

MAIN DISHES

Red Squirrel Stew

2-3 red squirrels (cleaned, cut in half crossways and soaked in salt water for an hour or so).
4 cups broth or bouillon
1 medium onion quartered
1 big handful of watercress (cleaned, leaves and stems can be found anytime of year. I had to break ice to get mine)
2 potatoes
1-2 carrots sliced
salt and pepper to taste

Put all ingredients in pot, put over fire and bring to boil. Remove from direct heat, set by fire and let simmer for 1-2 hours. Makes just enough for one real hungry outdoorsman!

Stuart L. Raymor • Belding, MI

Camper's Walleye Delight

fresh walleye or pike fillets
tomato and onion
HP sauce
soy sauce
ketchup
white wine

Spread a quarter inch of butter on large piece of aluminum foil. Lay row of fish fillets and cover with row of tomato slices. Then cover with row of onion slices. Another row of fish fillets. Another row of tomato slices and onion slices. Season to taste with sauces and wine, plus garlic salt very lightly sprinkled. Spread quarter inch of butter on another large piece of aluminum foil. Place it face down on the fish, and roll up corners with bottom foil. Place on canoe paddle and transport to grill under which a medium fire is going. Poke hole in foil top to let steam out. Let cook for about 15 minutes, taking care not to let too hot fire scorch the dish. Take off fire with paddle, transport to diners, cut open top of foil with knife, and ladle out the fish and delicious sauce still in foil.

Len Barnes • Editor, Michigan AAA Motor News

Hunter's Stew

1 pound ground beef
1 can (1 pound) tomatoes
½ cup water
1 teaspoon instant coffee powder
1 envelope (1¾ oz.) chili mix
1 can (1 pound) pork and beans

½ cup salted peanuts

Brown ground beef in large saucepan, stirring to crumble; drain excess fat. Stir in contents of chili mix envelope, tomatoes, pork and beans, water, peanuts and instant coffee. Bring to a boil, reduce heat and simmer uncovered for 10 minutes, stirring occasionally. 4 to 6 servings.

Mustard Grilled Fish

¼ cup mustard
1 teaspoon sugar
1½ to 2 pounds fish fillets or 4 to 6 small whole dressed fish
sliced bacon
¼ cup oil
½ teaspoon salt

Combine mustard, oil, sugar, salt and pepper. Wrap bacon around fish and fasten with food picks. Brush with mustard sauce. Grill 5 to 10 minutes. Turn, brush with sauce and grill 5 to 10 minutes longer. 4 to 6 servings.

Paul's "Stick to Your Ribs" Rice and Veggies Feast

The ingredients can be found at Natural Foods or Jewish grocery stores.
1 cup brown rice
⅓ ounce (weight) dried mushrooms, chopped
1 Telma brand mushroom soup cube
3 cups water (reserve ½ cup)
1 medium onion, chopped
1 Telma brand vegetable soup cube or 1 vegetable bouillon cube
½ cup dried vegetables or vegetable flakes
soy sauce or salt

Wash rice. Put rice in large pot with 2½ cups water. Bring to a boil. Reduce heat, and simmer covered for 50-60 minutes, never stirring. During the last 15 minutes, soak mushrooms in ½ cup water and saute onion in a little oil or butter. When rice is done, add all vegetable and soup bases. Toss lightly. Cover and let stand for 5-10 minutes so the vegetables rehydrate. Serves two hungry souls.

Bon appetit, pardner!

Paul A. Gutterman • East Lansing, MI

Hamburger Skillet Dinner

1½ pounds ground beef
1¼ cups cold water
½ teaspoon salt
1 1 pound can peas and carrots, drained
1 envelope onion gravy mix
½ cup cold milk
1⅓ cups mashed potato flakes
2 to 3 tablespoons butter

In medium skillet, combine meat and gravy mix. Cook over low heat until meat is done. Drain off fat. Make mashed potatoes by combining water, milk and salt. Add potato flakes and stir with fork. Pat meat along bottom and sides of skillet, like a crust. Spoon peas and carrots over crust. Spread mashed potatoes over the top. Cover and heat 15 to 20 minutes. 4 to 6 servings.

Bannock or Camp Bread

4 cups flour
⅓ cup water
1 teaspoon salt
4 teaspoons baking powder
6 tablespoons shortening

Mix ingredients thoroughly. Add just enough water until dough gathers into a ball. Press dough into round cake pan about one inch thick. Dust cake and coat frying pan with flour and drop cake into it. Bake in camp fire about 15 minutes. Test to see if it's done with wood splints—when the splinter comes out clean the bannock is done. No meal is complete without bread and no bread is better than bannock. It's as great at home as it is afield.

Mark Dilts • Outdoor writer, photographer

Planked Bass

Tack large fillets or a split whole bass to a strip of clean, bleached driftwood with skin side to the wood. Prop wood near the fire and brush fish frequently with hot strips of bacon or bacon drippings as they broil. Baste also with lemon if available. Season with salt and pepper. This is a leisurely method of cooking designed for a warm midday on a wilderness pond.

Camper's Covered Skillet Turkey

Cut turkey in pieces, fry until brown with butter, margarine or shortening. Drain off excess fat. Add one cup onions, chopped fine, one cup mushrooms, pepper, parsley if wanted and can of beer. Push back on the back of fire and let cook about 45 to 60 minutes at low heat.

Heap

bacon
eggs
boiled potatoes
onions

Cook bacon in frying pan and transfer ½ of the grease to a second pan for cooking fish. Hold bacon and break into small pieces. Slice and saute potatoes and onions in pan. Add eggs to suit and then add bacon. Serve with fish cooked crisp in second pan. Delicious and filling!

Whitefish in Foil

2 pounds whitefish fillets or other fish fillets, fresh or frozen
2 green peppers, sliced
2 onions, sliced
¼ cup butter or margarine, melted
dash pepper
2 tablespoons lemon juice
2 teaspoons salt
1 teaspoon paprika

Cut into serving-size portions. Cut 6 pieces of heavy-duty aluminum foil, 12 x 12 inches each. Grease lightly. Place a portion of fish, skin side down, on foil. Top with green pepper and onion. Combine remaining ingredients. Pour sauce over fish. Bring the foil up over the food and close all edges with tight double folds. Make 6 packages. Place packages on a grill about 5 inches from moderately hot coals. Cook for 45 to 60 minutes or until fish flakes easily when tested with a fork. Serves 6.

Campfire Smelt

3 pounds pan-dressed smelt or other small fish, fresh or frozen
2 teaspoons salt
⅓ cup chopped onion
3 strips bacon, cut in half
dash pepper
⅓ cup chopped parsley

Thaw frozen fish. Clean, wash and dry fish. Cut 6 pieces of heavy-duty aluminum foil, 12 x 12 inches each. Grease lightly. Divide fish into 6 portions. Place fish on foil. Sprinkle with salt and pepper. Place onion and parsley on fish. Top with bacon.

Bring the foil up over the food and close all edges with tight double folds. Make 6 packages. Place packages on a grill about 4 inches from hot coals. Cook for 10 to 15 minutes or until fish flakes easily when tested with a fork. Serves 6.

Poor Man's Fish

1 2 pound coffee can
favorite batter
2 forked sticks
fish
enough grease to fill can half full
1 piece of wire about 1½ ft. long
1 long straight stick

Take coffee can and punch a hole on each side of can about ½ inch from the top. Insert wire and twist together. After a fire is built take forked sticks and place into ground on each side of the fire. Fill the coffee can ½ full of grease, cooking oil or shortening. Place can over fire. When oil is hot place batter-dipped fish in until golden brown.

Bryce Wilson Berger • Bay City, MI

Foil Fish

Place a layer of chopped celery, sweet pepper and onions with fresh sliced tomatoes on a large piece of heavy-duty aluminum foil. Place a single layer of salmon or lake trout skinned and boned fillets on top of the foil. Add salt, pepper, two teaspoons of butter and Tabasco sauce. Add another layer of vegetables, another layer of fish with seasoning and another layer of vegetables. Fold the foil tightly to seal in the juices and steam and cook over a medium charcoal fire for 30 minutes. If the fish is flaky and tender and the vegetables aren't overcooked, you've done it just right.

Grilled Whole Fish

In a small saucepan, prepare a sauce consisting of:
¼ cup lemon juice and butter/oleo
½ teaspoon monosodium glutamate
1 drop salad oil
½ teaspoon garlic salt and dried oregano leaves
½ teaspoon soy sauce
2 tablespoons water
Heat on edge of cook-out grill.
Clean fish and score.
Adjust grill 5 inches from prepared coals. Place fish on greased strip of foil and grill for 12 to 15 minutes, turning once and brushing frequently with sauce.

Camp Chops

Provide lean, center cut chops cut thick. Place in a pan wide enough to accommodate all chops and leave room for turning. Season both sides with salt, cracked or ground pepper, ½ cup of chopped onions and freshly gathered sweet fern (this is not a real fern, but a short twiggy plant with fragrant, finely cut leaves, found near almost all north Michigan fishing areas).

Pour over the chops, one can of beer. The liquid should nearly cover the chops; water may be added unless you can spare another can of beer. Allow chops to marinate, turning occasionally for several hours. Cook on grill over steady heat about 15 minutes per side.

Pizza Stew

3 or 4 cube steaks, about 1½ pounds
2 tablespoons oil
1 envelope (1½ ounce) spaghetti sauce mix
1 can (6 ounce) tomato paste
1 cup pitted ripe olives, coarsely chopped
grated Parmesan cheese
4 green peppers
4½ cups water
1 cup uncooked elbow macaroni

Cut cube steaks and peppers in 1 inch cubes; brown in oil in large saucepan. Stir in water, contents of envelope of sauce mix, tomato paste, and macaroni. Cover and simmer 15 minutes, until macaroni is tender. Stir in ripe olives and cheese. Spoon into wide-mouthed vacuum jug. 6 servings.

Brisk and Bracing Beanpot

1 green pepper, cut up
1 pound frankfurters, sliced
1 can (1 pound, 4 ounce) pineapple tidbits
2 tablespoons brown sugar
1 tablespoon oil or melted shortening
2 cans (1 pound each) pork and beans
¼ cup prepared yellow mustard

Cook green pepper in oil in large skillet or saucepan until almost tender. Stir in frankfurters, pork and beans, undrained pineapple, mustard and brown sugar. Cook over medium heat, stirring occasionally, until bubbling hot. Spoon into vacuum jug. 8 servings.

DESSERTS

Minted Fridge Brownies

1 cup chopped walnuts
3 cups graham cracker crumbs
1 package (12 ounce) semi-sweet chocolate bits
1 cup undiluted evaporated milk
2 cups miniature marshmallows
1 cup sifted confectioners sugar
¾ teaspoon peppermint extract

Combine nuts, marshmallows, graham cracker crumbs and confectioners sugar in a large mixing bowl. Heat chocolate and evaporated milk in small saucepan over low heat, stirring constantly until blended. Remove from heat; stir in peppermint extract. Reserve ½ cup of the chocolate mixture, then mix the remainder with the graham cracker mixture until all crumbs are moistened. Spoon into well-buttered 9-inch square pan and press down to fit pan. Spread the reserved ½ cup chocolate mixture on top. Chill until ready to serve. Cut into 2-inch squares. Makes 16 squares. Make these at home to take along camping, for quick energy.

Fruit-Bread Pie

While coals heat, place pan on table or ground. Butter two slices of bread and place one slice butter side down in pan. Add liberal spoonful of fruit pie filling to top of bread slice, then cover with second bread slice, butter side up. Cover pan and place in hot coals, turning after five minutes.

MY RECIPES

Michigan United Conservation Clubs

*Here's a list of some of the ways
MUCC uses your membership dues...*

- Maintains a full-time legislative service providing information relating to conservation and environmental matters to the Legislature, Congress, the Governor's office, and state and federal agencies.
- Engages in legal suits to protect the state's natural resources.
- Supports hunting, fishing, and trapping as highly regarded forms of outdoor recreation.
- Conducts conservation and environmental education programs.
- Operates the MUCC Conservation Education Youth Camp.
- Serves as the official Michigan affiliate of the National Wildlife Federation.
- Publishes *Michigan Out-of-Doors*, a monthly magazine devoted to conservation and outdoor recreation. A part of your membership benefit.
- Publishes *Tuebor Terra*, a bimonthly magazine devoted to environmental issues affecting Michigan and the Great Lakes. A part of your membership benefit.
- Publishes *Tracks*, a monthly reader covering conservation subjects for elementary schoolchildren throughout the state.
- Monitors governmental, industrial, military, and other operations affecting natural resources.
- Conducts hunter safety training programs throughout Michigan.
- Conducts Wildlife Discovery, a conservation education program in classrooms in various parts of the state.
- Arranges conferences to train leaders in the conservation movement.
- Conducts the largest shotgun, rifle, pistol, and archery tournament in Michigan.
- Sponsors National Wildlife Week in Michigan.
- Informs the public regarding developments and issues on the conservation front.
- Presents Wildlife Encounters, a show using live animals to explain wildlife concepts.
- Coordinates National Hunting and Fishing Day in Michigan.
- Publishes books on conservation, map books, recreation guides, hydrographic maps, and other education materials relating to conservation and the outdoors.

*To become a member
see opposite page.*

*Thanks for putting your money
where your outdoor interests are.*

TUEBOR TERRA

the other publication of Michigan United Conservation Clubs.

Keep abreast of Michigan's environment, wildlife, and natural resources through *Tuebor Terra*, the nation's first statewide environmental watchdog magazine. It provides information you simply cannot find anywhere else about a region that is near and dear to you—Michigan. Find out what's happening to our breathtaking state. Read *Tuebor Terra*.

A one year membership with Michigan United Conservation Clubs includes six issues of *Tuebor Terra* for $25.00

Your dues for two years would be $40 and you will receive 12 issues.

michigan OUT-OF-DOORS

is America's largest state-specific, hunting, fishing, outdoor recreation and conservation magazine. Since its inception in January 1947, *Michigan Out-of-Doors* has evolved into a vibrant, glossy, four-color monthly publication that is considered the Great Lakes area's most consistent and influential voice for conservation and outdoor recreation.

What Is MUCC?

MUCC is the Michigan United Conservation Clubs, a statewide organization dedicated to further and advance the cause of the environment and conservation in all phases and to promote programs designed to educate citizens in natural resource conservation and environmental protection and enhancement.